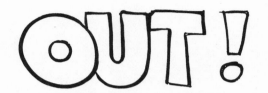

The Vermont Secession Book

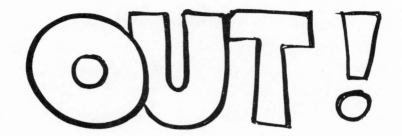

OUT!

The Vermont Secession Book

by
Frank Bryan and Bill Mares

Illustrated by Jeff Danziger

The New England Press
Shelburne, Vermont

ISBN 0-933050-52-6
Library of Congress Catalog Card Number: 87-62288
Design by Andrea Gray
Cover design by Jeff Danziger

For additional copies of this book or for a catalog
of our other New England titles, please write:

The New England Press
P.O. Box 575
Shelburne, Vermont 05482

This book is dedicated to our brothers:
David Bryan, Jan Mares, and Tom Mares.

ACKNOWLEDGMENTS

Among the many people who helped and encouraged us in writing this book, several co-conspirators deserve special mention: David Hale, Melissa Bryan, Chris Hadsel, Tom Slayton, Jeanne Bryan, Jeff Cederfield, Bill Ryerson, Norm Runnion, Vince Naramore, Sam Hand, Jim Pacy, John Downs, Glenn Gershaneck, Jim Fraser, Al Rosa, Paul Eschholz, and Jeff Olson.

Contents

A Vermont Parable

With a yoke of oxen, a man was skidding logs out of the woods. In the snow he lost the toggle bolt that held the loop of the chain that attaches the oxen to the heavy, log-laden sled. In an absentminded moment, he stuck in his finger to replace it.

"The steers hadn't more than begun to pull when I realized that I'd made a mistake."

A Special Note to the Reader

This book is about the coming secession of Vermont from the Union in 1991. It outlines many of the tactics and strategies that may be used in The Ultimate Great War of Secession, hereafter referred to as TUGWOS (pronounced *shoveit*). For that reason it is absolutely critical that:

THIS BOOK MUST NEVER FALL
INTO THE HANDS OF ANYONE
OUTSIDE THE STATE OF VERMONT.

Vermonters should use the utmost caution when traveling beyond Vermont's borders with this book. Preferably the contents should be memorized and the book left at home. It is imperative that it never appear:

1. Anywhere within a hundred-mile radius of G. Gordon Liddy.
2. In the hands of Teddy Kennedy.
3. On *The CBS Evening News*.
4. On the front page of *USA Today*.
5. In the possession of Muammar el-Qaddafi.
6. On Jane Fonda's bookshelf.
7. In Sylvester Stallone's car.
8. Anywhere within a fifty-mile radius of Washington, D.C.
9. In the editorial offices of *The New York Times*.
10. In Oliver North's briefcase.
11. On the coffee table of anyone living in New Hampshire or New York.

1

Red Dawn Over Vermont

(January 27, 1991, 6:31 A.M.)

Along the rim of New Hampshire's Mount Moosilauke to the east, a long red line appeared against the frost of a January dawn. It reminded Bill Mares of the desert – the color, the cold, the being alone. But riding a camel across Arabia was one thing; placing plastic explosives under the bridge linking Norwich, Vermont, and Hanover, New Hampshire, was another.

Odd. He didn't feel at all frightened as he eased his skinny runner's body down and under where the main strut caught the vapor from the river and turned it immediately to ice. In fact, a grin flashed through his own puffs of steam in the growing light. His fingers cooperated, too. They seemed immune to the temperature as he worked with pliers and wire fifty feet above where the swirling Connecticut River broke free of the ice and splashed against the bridge's great concrete pillars.

The grin was sparked by the thought of the havoc he was about to bring down on the many professors who taught at New Hampshire's Dartmouth College but lived across the river in Vermont. They said they paid the higher taxes in Vermont to escape the conservatism of New Hampshire. Bull. It was a nod to rural chic. Nice to be able to afford such a pretentious indulgence! And rural chic was over. Once this bridge and a dozen others like it went up around Vermont's border, everyone left in Vermont would have to come to grips with the real Vermont in a hurry! Well, there'd be a lot of missing professors this morning. And a lot of happy students.

But Bill's real delight originated deep within his soul, where a cosmic directive glowed at white heat. It read, *"You've always been a secessionist, Mares. And now you're going to blow this bridge into kingdom come, you hotshot son-of-a-bitch!"*

The very first ray of sunlight flashed down from the heights of the White Mountains toward the Connecticut River Valley and caught him right between the shoulder-blades as he trotted westward across the bridge. Mares the Montanan, Mares the Texan, Mares the world traveler, Mares the outdoorsman, Mares the Harvard grad and the ex-marine had finally come home. Home to the universal homeland. Home to Vermont. Home to help lead the greatest political movement on the North American continent since 1860.

He knew that somehow he should be thinking profound thoughts at such a moment. But all he could do was grin and imagine that bridge erupting into the cold New England dawn in an everlasting thunder of joy.

One hundred and twenty miles to the west, Frank Bryan was not only cold, he was scared shitless. Born on the *wrong* side — the eastern side — of the Connecticut River in New Hampshire (where he had lived for four days before his mother brought him home to Vermont's hospitalless town of Canaan), he now found himself on the wrong side of Lake Champlain, the now mostly frozen body of water that forms Vermont's western border with New York. The eastern glow he saw was over the Green Mountains of Vermont. They stretched, as Robert Frost had said, "extended straight" down the middle of the state, halfway between him and Mares.

"Crimus," muttered Bryan. "Born on the wrong side of the river, and I'll probably die on the wrong side of the lake. Like a Montanan dying in North Dakota or a Texan dying in Oklahoma."

He glanced wistfully toward Vermont. The few remaining patches of open water coughed up misty geysers of steam that weaved and danced ever so slowly in the icy wind. Bryan was always just a tad nervous when he was out of Vermont. But this . . .

His jackknife chattering between his teeth, he twisted the top from another half-gallon can of maple syrup. A bemittened hand grabbed the knife and popped the thin metal wafer from the mouth of the can. Then, turning it quickly upside down, he drove the knife into its shiny bottom, twisted it, and yanked it out. The air rushed in and the syrup gurgled sweetly out the other end and into the gas tank of still another armored personnel carrier owned by the United States Army.

Bryan didn't mind losing the syrup,[1] but he hated ruining all those perfectly good cans. Vermonters wasting syrup

[1] It was grade B. Grade A was being saved for popular consumption, and fancy grade would soon be pumped into the huge abandoned granite quarries in Barre to become the "liquid gold" that would support the state's new currency.

cans was like the people of India wasting cows or New York throwing away subway tokens.

Half an hour later, Operation Pancake was over, and the seventy-six vehicles of the 242nd Armed Assault Division were primed to go. Bryan figured they'd travel a mile, maybe two at the most, before their engines, sucking on that syrup-laced gasoline, would gum up, freeze, and grind to a halt forever.

Like Mares, he grinned. Unlike Mares, Bryan had never been east of Portland, Maine, in his life. He'd been thirty-three before he'd ever gone west of Albany or been up in an airplane. "Let Mares blow up his bridges," he muttered. It was more fun imagining the ultimate Vermont torture: the sounds of engines dying in the cold, of batteries slowly winding down. Errr-*urh*. Err-*uh*. Er—*UH!* He saw stiffened fingers dropping from ignition keys. He saw men slowly pounding their heads against frigid steering wheels while their frosty breath steamed against windshields. He saw bodies slumping in rage and resignation.

Finished, he headed back to the shore of the great lake, a solitary figure in the wide expanse of early morning frost. Twisting quickly to face the Adirondacks for a final time, he raised his fist on high and yelled fiercely into the wind, "That'll teach you Yorker bastards!" Then, forgetting his snowshoes, he turned for a dramatic leap toward a bright green John Deere snowmobile—and fell flat on his face.

A subdued "Crimus" tumbled out through the snow in his mouth as he struggled to get up.

No matter. It was a happy Frank Bryan who later gunned out across the lake toward a bright sun that sat, propped for a fantastic instant, on the peak of Lincoln Mountain—a green mountain—in the newly freed Republic of Vermont.

Elsewhere across Vermont the early light caught hundreds of shadowy figures briskly at work:

- The Darryl-Darryl Brigade, captained by Peter Smith (who liked the idea that as leader, he was the only one in the brigade allowed to talk), had cut off the access road to Killington Mountain, eastern America's largest ski resort. 23,276 flatlanders there and throughout Vermont would awaken to find themselves hostages of the new Republic.[2]

- High in the mountains above U.S. Route 9 a shadowy woodsman leaned on the handle of his peavy, ready to roll a log that would release 3,748,462 overripe zucchini (now lethally frozen) in an avalanche of seed, skin, and pulp. This would seal off the chief east-west transportation route across Vermont's southern border and (should the FUS [Former United States] government be crazy enough to try it) squash any attempt to move troops along the road below.

- The Olympic Brigade, led by silver medal winner Billy Kidd of Stowe and gold medal winner Barbara Cochran of Richmond, moved to capture communication towers atop Vermont's major mountains. Vermont's greatest deer hunter, Larry Benoit of Duxbury, was a member of this elite mountain division, too, because he could run up mountains faster than most people can ski down them. Christmas-tree baron Ernest "Stub" Earle (known as the Earle of Eden) had been allowed into the division but only after he agreed to reload his shotgun with rock salt. The Green Mountain Boys had freed Vermont from New York in the eighteenth century without killing anyone. Severing the United States from Vermont in the twentieth century would be done the same way.

- The Vermont Yankee nuclear power plant, situated on the Massachusetts border in Vernon, had been overrun

---

[2] Unfortunately, Smith had not counted on what later became known as the "red chief reverse." To facilitate crowd control, the hostages were allowed to continue to ski and make use of the resort's facilities. As the weeks passed, more and more of the "prisoners" refused to be ransomed. As long as snow conditions remained good, the only way to swap them for much-needed supplies from FUS (as the Former United States affectionately came to be called) was to bind them hand and foot and drag them off the mountain. Their screams angered the other prisoners and made the thinly manned garrison nervous.

at 3:45 A.M. by the Glow-Worm Platoon. Easily. Then three huge fans (six stories high and pointing south) were erected on the vapor-lighted grounds. The trucks arrived precisely on time, at 6:30, and the Republic's special Hill Farmer Brigade began unloading 16,418 bales of "hay" grown on seventy-three abandoned hill farms throughout Vermont that summer. Vermont State Senator Peter Welch began to pop them open by cutting the bale strings with a machete. With a crazed gleam in his eyes and a Perrier Lite in his free hand, he hashed and slashed, left and right.[3]

The first match was struck at 7:05. By 7:15, huge billows from the burning grass were rising into the frosty air, the great fans were engaged, and clouds of odd-smelling smoke began drifting southward over New England. For once the weather cooperated, and by 8:45 there were very few people in western Massachusetts who gave a sweet damn whether Vermont had seceded from the Union or not.

More important (and precisely according to plan), when the 246,000 college students who attended schools from Orono to New York eventually got wind of what was going on and headed toward the Vermont border, they completely immobilized highway traffic on the eastern seacoast for two days.

Bernie Sanders, the socialist ex-mayor of Vermont's largest city and the man who commanded the grassroots crew of farmers that staffed the Hill Farmer Brigade, leaned over a tiny radio in his command post in Burlington.[4] At 10:36 A.M. the announcement crackled through as if from some far distant planet. His ex-Honor the Mayor turned to the hushed cadre of hill farmers with the anxiously awaited code words for success at Vernon:

---

[3] Observers at the scene reported later that he kept muttering happily to himself, "Take that Poirier, take that Guest — and that — and that."

[4] Located in the vault in the City Clerk's Office on Church Street.

"Comrades," he said solemnly, "the Vermont Yankee nuclear power plant has been turned on."

- The interstate highway system posed a special danger to the new republic. These long, winding snakes of concrete and asphalt provided a direct route to the very heartland of Vermont should it be invaded from the south — in this case by FUS. But the federal designers of the highway system made one key error. They built tall sturdy fences along the road banks, presumably to keep Vermont's dairy cows from wandering onto the highway. But fences built to keep critters *out* can also be used to keep critters *in*. By 9:45 A.M. of January 27, 1991, every dry cow, heifer, beef cow, calf and steer in Vermont — all 272,714 of them — had been herded onto the interstate by units of the Hill Farmer Brigade. By 2:30 that afternoon, the pavement had become too slippery for travel by wheeled vehicles. An overflight by the FUS Air Force at 2:45 looked down and saw, stretched far into the horizon, miles and miles of contented cattle standing or lying sleepily on both lanes in the afternoon sun, chewing their cuds, and now and then lifting their tails. They also saw tractor-hauled wagons rolling down the center lines while members of the FFV[5] tossed off bales of real hay for the evening feeding. From the cockpit of a low-flying F-111, a young lieutenant in the FUS Air Force radioed his astonishment back to base: "Holy Cow!"
- Only two maneuvers were botched on that cold January morning. Senator Madeleine Kunin (who was named to Senator Patrick Leahy's U.S. Senate seat in 1989 when Leahy was named Director of Leak Control under President Haig) had been chosen to lead the Tweener Brigade; her first assignment was to find Supreme Court Justice John Dooley and ask him what to do. Unfortunately, despite secret planning on the part of her staff, her Brigade encountered a fork in the road, either branch of

[5] Future Farmers of Vermont.

which would have taken it safely to its destination. At 9:48 A.M. Kunin's Tweener Brigade was still waiting at the crossroads while she tried to make up her mind which road to take. At 10:30, after a hastily named study committee became deadlocked, she issued a clear-cut decision. The Brigade would take *both* roads. Kunin then named a study committee to decide which half of the Brigade should take which branch. At 12:15 Madeleine was upbeat. Her second committee was about to report its findings, and she was certain that the Tweener Brigade would soon be under way.

Vermont's lone congressman, Jim Jeffords,[6] also behaved true to form. For years he had been able to convince Vermonters that a confused record in Washington was really an "independent" record. That first day of TUGWOS he was eager to act on his own again. With a band of his loyal followers he charged off to hijack Amtrak's Montrealer as it passed through Bellows Falls at dawn. Thirteen hours later he still stood shivering on the station platform looking wistfully down the tracks toward the south. Jeffords was saved from a night in subzero temperatures by Deacon Dundu of Athens who walked by at 7:15 P.M. and said, "If you're waitin' fer the train, it hasn't come by here since nineteen hundred and eighty-seven. Don't you ever pay attention to what's going on in Washington?"

• The contents of 143 liqua-store silos were pumped into tank trucks and driven to the banks of the Connecticut and Hoosic Rivers. The latter is a chief tributary of the Hudson. The former flows through the heart of New England and into Long Island Sound. Members of the Hill Farmer Brigade stood by the spigots. If FUS got feisty with Vermont, they were prepared to stink over thirty million innocent civilians along the eastern seaboard out of their ever-loving minds.

[6] Who had returned to the House after a quixotic run for the Senate against Bill Gray in 1988.

- Finally, all television and radio stations were immediately nationalized. At 7:48 regular programming ceased, and a brief announcement was heard telling Vermonters what ninety-eight percent of them had known for weeks: Vermont was throwing out "the other forty-nine" and going it alone. Country music albums were played on the radio, and reruns of *Hee Haw* appeared on local television stations.

2

Rather Dan Goes to Work

A telephone call awoke Mr. Dan early on January 27, 1991. Dan's boss, the president of CBS, was distraught. His voice quavered.

"Get down here right now, Rather! We've got one that's going to make Watergate and Iranamuck look like DAR conventions."

"What is it this time?" Rather grumbled.

"Vermont has seceded from the Union."

Rather Dan hung up in disgust, buried his head in the pillow, and muttered something about lunatics. The morning shift at the office dearly loved to waken him with crackpot comments: "Nancy Reagan has defected," "Henry Kissinger and Jeane Kirkpatrick are engaged." But he had to admit that this was one of their better lines. Vermont leaving the Union. Sure, and I'm Buffalo Bill.

But at 10:30, when Rather Dan interrupted *The Price Is Absurd* with a CBS Special Report, he didn't feel at all like laughing anymore. In fact, it was a trembling, ashen-faced Rather Dan that looked out at America and said:

"Vermont has seceded from the Union.

"Little is known at this time," he continued. "The only formal announcement of this incredible act CBS News has at this time is a message from a radio transmitter from someplace called Victory, which according to our map is a tiny village in Vermont near the Canadian border. We monitored the message at 8:10 this morning. It reads:

'GOOD MORNING, AMERICA.
VERMONT SAYS STICK IT IN YOUR EAR.
WE'RE SECEDING.
WE WON'T MAKE THAT MISTAKE AGAIN!' "

Rather Dan was suddenly struck by the fact that what he was saying was monstrously crazy. He wasn't going to be *believed*. Abandoning a ream of notes about exploding bridges, broken communications, sabotaged army vehicles, the seizure of a nuclear power plant, and even the use of chemical warfare in the form of great clouds of marijuana drifting over the East Coast, he looked squarely into the camera with the little red light and gasped for breath. Then he said in an earnest whisper:

"It's true, folks. I swear it. So help me Cronkite."

3

The Moscow Covenant

On December 20, 1980, the Trapp Family Lodge, located near the tiny village of Moscow, Vermont, burned to the ground. Winkin Jones, a Christmas-tree cutter from Waterbury, was helping with the cleanup when he noticed, under one of the ancient fieldstone slabs that had made up the foundation, a small iron box. Winkin didn't know the history of the Trapp Family—the escape from Nazi Europe or the famous musical *The Sound of Music* based on that event. But like most Vermonters he figured all resort owners were very rich.

That was why he came back to the cellar hole later that night and made off with the box. If he hadn't, no one would ever have discovered the real truth about the birth of America and Vermont's role in it. When Winkin smashed open the old box with a splitting maul, he found no money but two documents, brittle with age and written in a script that was nearly indecipherable.

Winkin, disappointed, gave the papers to his son Blinkin. The latter, a student at the University of Vermont and the first in his family to go to college, shared them with one of his professors who taught Vermont history.

The professor was in a hurry. He told Blinkin to Xerox a copy and put it on his desk, promising to look it over within a few days. In the meantime he suggested that Blinkin turn the originals over to the state archivist. But Blinkin left them in his brother Nod's pickup truck. That was where they were when Nod Jones tried some early ice fishing on Lake Champlain. Neither he nor the truck was recovered until spring. In their grief for Nod, Winkin and Blinkin forgot all about the documents. The professor did too, until the copies turned up four years later (in 1987) when he was giving his office its bi-decade cleaning.

What were these papers? They were a record of the most important agreement ever reached by Americans, even more significant than the federal Constitution itself, for the agreement allowed Vermont to throw the other states out of the Union anytime it wished.

From the time of its discovery, the document has been called the Moscow Covenant. This covenant was a secret accord reached by Ethan Allen and George Washington in January 1789 in Hackensack, New Jersey. Its contents have been made known to only a select group of Vermonters over the decades. But all true Vermonters have always sensed its existence, and have followed its dictates when the need arose.

No one knows why the Moscow Covenant was not made public in 1889 (as was allowed by the document's terms) or how the original document ended up in Moscow. But one thing is clear. Vermont's instinctual capacity to do the right thing and to provide moral leadership for the nation can now be explained.

The reason George Washington signed the original thirteen colonies over to Vermont is also simple to explain: The Vermont Constitution, which was the most liberal constitution on the North American continent at the time of its writing and the first to outlaw slavery, came into conflict with the proposed federal Constitution, which recognized blacks as property, not people. During the

Hackensack negotiations, in which Ethan Allen and George Washington sought to discover a way to bring Vermont and America together, Allen refused to concede Vermont's position on slavery. Washington, a good man himself, was so impressed and shamed by Allen's impassioned defense of the proposition that blacks were people that he agreed to sign a covenant that placed the sovereignty of the Union in Vermont's hands.[1] Vermont would then publicly "join" the Union in 1791 to make FUS look good. Why else would Vermonters have ratified the U.S. Constitution 109–4 at Bennington in 1791?

The existence of this document has long been suspected. Greg Sanford, Vermont state archivist, reports that several times a year he gets calls from antinukers, gun nuts, and civil rights activists from around the United States asking about the "escape clause" in the Vermont Constitution. Allegedly, this clause permits the state to withdraw from the Union under sufficient provocation. Patiently, Sanford explains that no such clause exists. Nor, Sanford adds, is there a "Brigadoon Clause" that permits the state every hundred years to review its membership in the Union and, if sufficiently provoked, to secede.

We now know that these critical passages are found in the secret Moscow Covenant and *not* in the state constitution.[2] Discovered and preserved by the Joneses of Waterbury, it reads as follows:

[1] The signing took place in January of 1789 during the great "black hole" of American history: six days for which there is no historical record of the American government doing anything and George Washington's whereabouts is unknown. Allen's death came only days later (February 12, 1789) when he collapsed after a night of raucus partying. The story of his death has oft been told. The discovery of the Moscow Covenant has revealed the cause of the celebration.

[2] One might wonder why a covenant formed in Hackensack but found near Moscow is named after Moscow. The answer is simple: Who ever heard of a "Hackensack Covenant," for Pete's sake.

The Moscow Covenant

Whereas no Vermont man will countenance in any way, form or manner any diminution or usurpation of his inalienable rights;

Whereas Vermont has signally demonstrated its transcendent moral leadership in the community of nations through its magnanimous manumission of all slaves;

Whereas the United States, through its continued acquiescence in this repugnant, repellent, and vicious practice, has earned the obloquy and condemnation of all free men;

Whereas Vermont has never recognized the courts, laws, legal officers, civil or military, of Crown or Congress but rather derived its powers according to the sacred rites of free men;

Whereas Vermont has attained the sublimest pinnacle of human endeavor and ought to secure the future blessings as just rewards for its glorious past;

Whereas Vermont has secured for its citizens perfect liberty against the vicissitudes of fortune and the deceits of its neighbors;

Therefore, be it agreed that I, George Washington, hereby grant my word and my honor to the union of the United States and the Republic of Vermont, hereafter to be known as the Green Mountain Federation;

And that in this action I have the verbal assent of Congress (taken in a secret session by an unrecorded voice vote);

That I certify and warrant that certain anti-Federalists such as Thomas Jefferson have also agreed to this Covenant;

That in the ordinary course of human events and governance, the United States Congress shall rule.

However, two exceptions shall always obtain and rend the Firmament in their clarity:

First, as the conscience of the United States, Vermont has the inalienable right to declare null and void and thereby ignore and avoid any law of the United States it wishes, and

Second, if at any time the United States fails to satisfy Vermont's high standards of probity, generosity, morality, and sobriety, Vermont may banish the United States from its borders forever.

Both parties agree to keep this Covenant secret for at least one hundred years.

Signed,

Ethan Allen

Ethan Allen

George Washington

George Washington

There it is, the Moscow Covenant, Vermont's ticket to freedom. But it was much more. It was Vermont's chance to preserve the soul of the federal Constitution, to be the steward of the American conscience, the heartland of the nation. As such it provided the conceptual glue that held together the principal events of Vermont history. Consider the following:

- For fourteen years before joining the Union, Vermont was an independent Republic.
- Vermonters did more to start the war with the British than did Paul Revere or the Minutemen at Lexington and Concord. They captured the largest British fort in North America long before the Continental Congress was actually committed to armed warfare. The English, understandably, were rip-shit.
- Having started the war, Vermont later finished it at the Battle of Hubbardton, which they won by losing. Hubbardton, a rearguard action on a hillside in western Vermont, bought time for the Colonists to regroup for the victory at Bennington (a Vermont battle fought by mistake in New York). This led to the victory at Saratoga, which led to the French entry into the War,

which led to the surrender of Cornwallis at Yorktown. Vermont always finishes what it starts.

- Vermont, while fighting hard for the Colonies, kept its options open. It even negotiated with Canada during the war. Did Vermont really want to become a province? Only one thing is clear. Vermont never intended to surrender its sovereignty to anyone.

- After the Revolution, Vermont coined its own money, raised its own army, put down internal rebellions, and went it alone as an independent Republic.

- During its years as a free nation Vermont set its own course. Believing it was destined for Great Power status, the Republic reached out to claim lands from part of much of present New Hampshire and a big chunk of New York. Vermont eventually rescinded this action. The world still believes that it caved in under pressure from the United States in anticipation of being admitted to the Union as the fourteenth state. The truth, of course, is that this action was only a sop to George Washington, who had signed over the entire United States of America to Vermont at Hackensack only days earlier.

- It was during this period that Ethan Allen, the warrior hero of Vermont's early beginnings, looked the Congress straight in the eye and issued the now famous proclamation:

I am as determined to preserve the Independence of Vermont as Congress is that of the United States and rather than fail I will retire with my hardy green mountain boys into the caverns of the mountains and make war on all mankind.[3]

Americans are even more ignorant of the independence Vermont demonstrated when she allowed the Colonies to join her in the new Green Mountain Federation of 1789. Reading the Moscow Covenant, it is obvious that Vermont always considered itself free and allowed the semblance of national leadership to continue only because of the heretofore secret promise George Washington made to Ethan Allen at Hackensack. How else can one explain the following:

- Before the U.S. Constitution was even fifteen years old, a Vermont congressman openly defied a law passed by Congress (the evil Sedition Act), was jailed for doing so, and was reelected to Congress *while in jail* in Vergennes. Money to pay his fine came from as far away as Virginia. It is hard to explain Mathew Lyons's acts by anything other than the Moscow Covenant, which stipulated that no Vermonter must ever obey a federal law repugnant to the Vermont Constitution, as the Sedition Act most certainly was!
- For the most part, the Green Mountain State chose to ignore the War of 1812 and carried on a brisk trade with Canada throughout. Vermont cattle poured through "Smuggler's Notch" to feed the British army in Canada.
- Vermont continued to react whenever the federal government broke the Moscow Covenant. Of all the northern states, for instance, Vermont sponsored the most sophisticated underground railroad. We simply ignored the Fugitive Slave Act, as of course we had every right to

[3] The fact that Vermont's mountains lack caves big enough to house even a squad of soldiers was not fully realized at the time. This problem was easily solved during TUGWOS. Troops were hidden in Vermont's 115 covered bridges. One minute they were marching down the highway. The next minute they were gone.

do. Vermont Supreme Court Justice Theophilus Herrington, when ordered to return a fugitive slave, demanded (in one of the greatest TUGWOS gestures of all time) "a Bill of Sale from the Almighty" before he would do so.

- Once it became apparent that the southern states were not about to give up slavery, Vermont unleashed its full fury on the slaveholding states of the South. Historian Earle Newton reports some of the bitterness that ensued:

> Georgia demanded that a ditch be dug around Vermont and that the pestiferous state be floated out to sea. As late as 1880 a southern newspaper suggested that the nation trade off Vermont to Canada "in payment of some ancient fish indemnity" or that at least it "be put on exhibition, as a fossil annex, at some future world's fair, if well fenced in and properly guarded."

- Vermont continually warned that the Moscow Covenant could not abide slavery. In 1848 Vermont's governor announced, "Vermont has taken the ground of irreconcilable hostility, and she must and will continue to maintain it."
- In 1850 the Vermont legislature once again demonstrated its understanding that Vermont was an independent force among the nations by passing the following resolution: "The brave and patriotic people of Hungary are entitled to our warmest sympathy in their unsuccessful struggle for their liberty against the despots of Austria and Russia."
- Vermont spent more money and gave more lives per capita during the Civil War than any other state.[4] But the motivation was not so much to preserve the sanctity of the federal Constitution (which had been superseded by the Moscow Covenant in 1789 anyway) as to free the slaves.
- In 1867 Vermont was the staging point for an army of

[4] Some historians claim Michigan may share that distinction, but we doubt it.

two thousand Irish Fenians who charged across the border to Canada from Franklin, Vermont, as the advance forces of an Irish-American army for the liberation of Ireland. Vermont's complicity in this attack in direct defiance of United States marshals was the act of a sovereign state.

- In 1917 Vermont appropriated one million hard-earned bucks for battle against Germany—before the federal government declared war. It also established the policy of paying Vermont troops in the United States Army an extra salary.[5]

- When Vermont was devastated by a catastrophic flood in 1927, President Calvin Coolidge, himself a real Vermonter, offered the state federal aid. Governor John Weeks refused. Standing amid the rubble of the state's worst natural disaster in all its history, he proudly informed an astonished America, "Vermont will take care of its own."

- During the Depression in a statewide referendum taken at town meeting, Vermonters voted down a huge federal parkway designed to ride the ridge line of the Green Mountains from Massachusetts to Canada. It would have been the greatest public works project ever attempted in Vermont, bringing with it chests of Union gold and tremendous economic development. But Vermont did not want its mountains "hitched together" (as historian Ralph Nading Hill put it) or blacktopped. Most of all, we didn't want them tarnished by federal money or federal control. "Take your asphalt and TUGWOS," we said.

[5] Vermont was so independent of Washington in its activities against Germany even before America joined the war that *The Burlington Free Press* was moved to write a series of editorials cautioning Vermont not to try to finance the war itself, that we had no responsibility to bail out a United States that was militarily bankrupt; and that, if we did insist on financing part of the war effort all by ourselves independently of the United States, we should raise taxes to do so, not float a bond issue, which would only mortgage the future of women and children. Again, Vermont was acting true to form—as an independent nation.

- In September 1941, three months before the Japanese attack on Pearl Harbor, the Vermont legislature passed a law that some historians claim was tantamount to a declaration of war on the Axis powers.[6] This suggests that Franklin Roosevelt was working with the secret trustees of the Moscow Covenant in Vermont to bring America into World War II as soon as possible.[7]

Taken individually these events are lost in the vast march of history. But seen under the incandescent glow of the Moscow Covenant, the awesome truth strikes home like an August thunderclap:

VERMONT NEVER JOINED THE UNION; THE UNION JOINED VERMONT.

---

[6] Historian Ralph Nading Hill put it bluntly: "In 1941 Vermont declared war on Japan before Washington did." Actually, what we did was pass a law to provide extra salary for any Vermonter fighting in the upcoming war to augment that paid by the national government.

[7] The fact that Vermont was only one of two states to vote against FDR in 1936 was obviously a cleverly designed ruse to camouflage Roosevelt's relationship with the Covenant.

4

One Too Many Tugs on the Teat

February 4, 1991
(TUGWOS Plus 8)
The Old Stone House
Brownington

A blinding snow squall slashed the hills of Vermont's Northeast Kingdom. Like giant hawks, four helicopters settled to the ground near the Old Stone House, searchlights playing here and there across the face of a premature twilight.

Through the dusk and the billows of snow kicked up by the alien craft, Lieutenant Colonel Bentley Bentley, USMC, a special envoy from the President of the United States, hurried across the snow, surrounded by three staff assistants, four armed guards, a half-dozen Secret Service agents, and several specialists on international relations. Out of the bowels of two of the helicopters, fifty-six Special Forces troopers rushed to take up positions around the building, weapons at the ready. Bentley Bentley was not happy. No one had told him Vermont's Revolutionary Council had moved its headquarters from Victory to Brownington, and he had spent the day asking directions and getting a lot of smartassed replies. The colonel burst through the door of the Old Stone House.

"What the *hell* is going on here!" he bellowed. "You hillbillies may not know it, but President Alexander Haig is *still in charge* of this government of ours!"

"In charge of *your* government, don't you mean?" said Madeline Harwood, former Vermont state senator and newly chosen co-chairperson of Vermont's Revolutionary Council.

"I'm not so sure he's in charge of that one, either," muttered Sallie Soule, former state Commissioner of Employment and Training, the other co-chairperson. The nine-member Council sat at a long table strategically positioned near a huge old wood stove, which cracked and spat its own objections.

Bentley strode menacingly toward the front of the room, his entourage arrayed behind him. "Listen, I represent the government of the United States, and—"

"Hush," said Madeline. "You don't have the floor, sergeant. Now, brush off that snow and tell those nice boys standing around outside to come in before they catch their death. No, no, no"—she raised her hand to silence Bentley—"I won't have it. The Grange has prepared coffee and doughnuts. You fellows sit down and get warm, then we'll talk."

An hour later the contingent from FUS—soldiers, statesmen, diplomats, and copter pilots—seemed more in control of themselves. Outside, the helicopters had been shut down and were slowly disappearing under the snow. Across the way, farmer Bill Ketchner was milking his Guernseys. A Special Forces private from Georgia was talking cows with the husband of one of the ladies in the Grange. Anthony Morehead, special counsel to President Haig, was dozing by the stove.

Harwood brought the meeting to order. "I understand President Haig is upset," she began.

"Upset, Madeline? Upset? He's pi . . ." Bentley Bentley paused and looked down at Jennifer Brown, a four-year-old cuddled in her mother's lap next to him. "Upset," he said quietly.

"And," said Sallie Soule, noticing Bentley's chagrin, "you must be recognized to speak, Sergeant Bentley. So watch it."

"Don't know rules of order, does he?" came a mutter from the end of the table. "There ain't no town meetings in Washington."

Bentley sighed, mumbled something about being a colonel, and took another bite of his fourth homemade doughnut. Damn, these were good. Looking around the room, he wished his people would at least *act* interested. But most of them seemed, well, relaxed and happy as the snow rapped against the windows of the Old Stone House now and then. His band of forty-two Special Forces troopers were in a corner playing cards or talking quietly with several locals who had roared up on snowmobiles for no apparent reason.

Bentley began again. "But *why,* Madeline? *Why* did Vermont secede from the Union?" he asked almost plaintively. "What have you got against the United States?" His eyes flashed quietly to one of his assistants, who understood the order immediately and got up to get Bentley another doughnut.

"You threw one too many bales onto the wagon, sergeant," answered Madeline.

"What?"

"Yeah, you put too many stones on the boat," explained someone else.

"You heaped one too many forkfuls on the spreader," said Sallie Soule.

"Took one too many tugs on the teat!" yelled Bill Ketchner, who had finished milking.

Madeline smiled approvingly. "We anticipated that question, sergeant. Accordingly, we asked the Barton chapter of the DAR to sponsor an essay contest on the subject. Alfred Le Croix, a dairy farmer from Coventry, is here to read his winning essay, 'Good-bye to FUS.' Of course, it doesn't reflect all our opinions, exactly." She smiled at Bentley Bentley. "But we feel it's a fair answer to your question. Now, would you fellows like another cup of coffee before Alfred begins?"

From over in the corner one of the thirty-eight Special Forces troops said, "Yup." A short time later a nervous Alfred Le Croix got up, cleared his throat, and addressed the meeting.

GOOD-BYE TO FUS

For two centuries Vermonters have put up with a lot from America. Too much. Our association with the United States has caused an accumulation of offenses matched only by our capacity to forgive, to accept hollow apologies, and to begin (we are ashamed to admit) to question our own principles in an attempt to go halfway and look at things through others' eyes.

Enough. We have probed our conscience. There is only one conclusion to be reached:

YOU HAVE TRASHED THE MOSCOW COVENANT. OUT YOU GO.

We've allowed millions of Americans to tramp the state scaring our cows, taking our pictures, getting lost in our woods, driving into our ditches, and tempting us with their bankrolls. We've consoled our cows, kept the landscape clean for their cameras, formed rescue squads to find them, hauled them out of ditches, and spent their money as fast as possible.

We've let America bore the hell out of us with its never-ending presidential elections.[1] We watched quietly as national TV news programs were transmogrified into entertainment. Watergate, Billygate, Irangate, Tailgate? Why not be honest and call the nightly news *Good Evening America*? We've even allowed the sale of *USA Today* in Vermont.

[1] We knew America was in trouble when the wisest bumper sticker to come out of the 1984 presidential election read, VOTE FOR MONDALE — AT LEAST YOU'LL LIVE TO REGRET IT.

We've let America bug us, sell us, invest us, and deceive us. We've let it draft us and stink us and tax us and then blame us. We've let it rate our movies. We're sick of television tripe named after cities like Dallas and Miami and Houston. We're fed up with wondering what the difference between PG and PG-13 is. We're even disgusted with ourselves because we worry about worrying.

What's authentic, anyway? Do world crises dance only to the tune of network ratings? What's the real news? Whatever happened to the environmental crisis? World famine? Was there an energy crisis in the 1970s or not? Is a nuclear freeze less important now than it was ten years ago?[2] Will the real America please stand up?

And what about leadership? What were our choices in the last presidential election? The self-righteous Jesse Jackson? George Bush, who called Reagan's policies "voodoo economics" but then signed on as a medicine man in the Reagan circus? Teddy Kennedy? Gary Hart? *Haig?* Mario Cuomo, the Italian Hamlet?

Vermonters remember the story about the Lone Ranger and Tonto. The two are cornered by a band of Indians. The Lone Ranger cries out to Tonto, "What are we going to do?" And Tonto says, "What do you mean *we,* white man?"

Pogo was wrong. We have met the enemy, and he is *not* us. The enemy is you guys, and we're leaving.

We're tired of threats, too.

- Lower your speed limit.
- Raise your speed limit.
- Adjust your drinking age, or we won't give you your own tax money back.
- Pass a seatbelt law, or we'll mandate air bags.
- Improve your schools, or the Japanese will bury you.

[2] Vermont tried desperately to get America moving on this issue in the early 1980s when over 150 of our towns demanded a nuclear arms freeze. President Reagan snickered. The country perked up for a while. The media paid attention for a bit. Then it was over. Apparently it didn't sell in prime time. The nation got bored. We didn't.

- Save energy, or have a war in the Persian Gulf.
- Buy SDI, or be taken over by the Soviets.

For years you've misunderstood us, calling us Republican and conservative. Then in the 1980s you started calling us Democrats. We are none of the above. We are *conservationists*. We like to *conserve* things, like clean air, clean water, democracy, and common decency. We *like* governments—the more, the merrier. But we like them to be of *appropriate* size. We want to be able to get our hands on them. Most of all, we want politicians we can believe.[3] America has given up on democracy. We haven't. We tried to tell you a thousand times. But you wouldn't listen. Well, maybe you'll pay attention to this: *Get lost!*

HYPOCRISY HAS BECOME AMERICA'S MIDDLE NAME, AND WE'RE FED UP WITH IT.

- Billy Graham was suspect for urging the worship of Jesus Christ, while Timothy Leary was a hero for worshiping the use of LSD.
- Bobby Kennedy was applauded for "tough political maneuvering," while Richard Nixon was an evil man for doing the same thing.

[3] Vermonters *felt* the sting of William F. Buckley's remark in the late 1960s that went something like this: "They told me that if I voted for Barry Goldwater, there would be rioting in the streets and America would end up in a war in Asia. I voted for Goldwater and, sure enough, there were and we did."

- It is okay to slaughter thousands of calves and lambs every day for America's chic restaurants, but it's cruel and inhuman for a working-class Canadian to kill seal pups so he can afford hot dogs and beans.
- Why do Washington politicians look for poverty nine hundred miles away in Mississippi when it flourishes on their doorsteps?
- America salves its conscience about hunger by having beautiful people (who work off more calories every day at expensive health clubs than most of the world's poor consume) sing a few songs, claim they are "the world," and then go back to their high-living ways while surplus food continues to rot in American warehouses.
- The federal government spends our money to subsidize tobacco growers one day and spends more of our money urging us not to smoke the next. What's going *on* here?

Why couldn't you have given it to us straight? We want to do the right thing. But the more we do the right thing, the worse things get.

Is the family in or out? How many children should we have? You told us that if we "planned" our families, we'd have better families. We did, and we haven't. Do you want our farmers to produce more milk or less? Is space the final frontier or a wastebasket for broken dreams? Do the Soviets want to bury us or not? Are the contras winning or losing? Who do honest folks that want to do right believe?

We've seen too much! We've seen everything from wrenches to men's shirts be sold with sex. In 1987 barges full of garbage cruised America's coast looking for a place to land. That was one time Vermont was glad it didn't have a seacoast.

Alfred Le Croix paused and took a deep breath. It was warm by the stove, and he was excited. But when he looked up at the group before him, he noticed something strange. It was dead quiet. The thirty-six Special Forces were listening attentively from the rear. Some of Bentley

Bentley's assistants were leaning forward in their chairs. One of them raised his eyebrows at a colleague as a sign of approval. The colonel pretended not to notice all this and yawned. But inside, his guts told him, *Haig's got trouble. Deep trouble.*

Le Croix continued:

Our premise is simple: Vermonters can do it better themselves. We are better at education, welfare, building roads, catching crooks, dispensing justice, and helping farmers. We report our own news better. Vermonters know much more about what's happening in Vermont than Americans know about what's happening in America. We're better at democracy, too, much better. We can balance our budget! We've watched as Congress pitters and patters, dillies and dallies, postures, poses, and primps. If that's America's idea of democracy, we want out!

Patience? We've been so damned patient.

- Did we toss out the other forty-seven when the United States became the first and only nation to use atomic weapons by dropping two on residential cities in Japan just to show them we could?
- Did we dismiss the other states and dissolve the Union when America failed to join the League of Nations?
- Did we pull out when President Jack Kennedy trained a secret army and invaded Cuba in 1961? Remember the Bay of Pigs? Talk about secret arms deals—how about secret armies?
- Did we jettison America when President Nixon brought national shame to us all and trashed the presidency?
- Have we declared war on Ohio, Indiana, Illinois, and Kentucky for drenching us with acid rain?
- We resisted our urge to conduct protective reaction air strikes against *The Manchester Union Leader,* did we not?
- Did we bail out when Ronald Reagan dumped James Watt as interior secretary and replaced him with Donald Hodel?

- Did we revolt when you coerced us into raising our drinking age to twenty-one—even though the Constitution absolutely forbids you to make policy in this area—or you'd take away our highway funds? We sued you. We should have done more. Now we have.
- Did we go it alone when the United Nations accepted nation after nation with less population than Vermont?
- In 1988 you elected Alexander "I'm in Charge" Haig President. We like Ollie North too, but as secretary of state? Sure Nixon opened up China, but did Haig need to name him ambassador to China? Is Henry Kissinger really the best man for secretary of health and human services?

- Did we abandon the other forty-nine states when the Air Force paid $765.28 apiece for dental floss dispensers in 1989?

We Are History

In the 1980s America made several especially hurtful yanks on our patience. Congress, in one of the most devious, despicable, dastardly displays of dishonesty in the history of dirty deals, raised its own pay while voting to do otherwise. I am not going to spell out the procedure for fear you would barf all over this nice old building.[4] But the real horror was the apathy with which America greeted the news: "Ho hum, that's the way it is in Washington." Or, "That's politics." Even in Vermont some were so deadened to the ubiquitous cynicism that they uttered only a tired "Those sneaky bastards."

Then rural mail carriers were told not to deliver incorrectly addressed mail—even if (get *this*) the carrier had known the occupant all his or her life. The specter of neighbors being told not to deliver their neighbors' mail was one yank too many on a very sore subject.

And when the Montrealer went off the track in Essex Junction, killing several, one major network reported that the accident occurred "somewhere in Vermont fifteen miles east of Plattsburgh, New York." Fifteen miles east of *Plattsburgh*! Crimus! *Now* do you know where Vermont is—now that we ain't there anymore?

The Final Tug

But the final tug on the teat—the one that made the pail fly—was when *USA Today* came to Vermont and held a "town meeting" in Burlington's Radisson Hotel to find out how people spend their money. Talk about money-changers in the temple! Burlington isn't even a town! There were no votes taken; no Warning was issued. Not one officer's report was read. No town officers were thrown out. None were elected. No homemade pie was served. They didn't

[4] All right, I'll tell you how they did it. But first get yourself a pail. First of all, Congress removed itself from the process of raising its own salaries by having President Reagan do it. It did this by requiring that whenever the bureaucracy got a raise from the President, senators and congressmen would, too. Neat trick. But in the law setting this up, it allowed itself the right to disapprove the raise if it did so within a given number of days. After that time the raise would be automatic. On the evening of the last day to deny itself a raise in 1987, Congress postponed the debate until the next day, when its right to do so would be gone. Then the next day—you got it—it voted to deny itself the raise even though it was too late to do so. Can you believe that? And they knew America would put up with it. Well, America did, but we won't.

even elect their own moderator. In short, nothing happened except talk.

If *USA Today* doesn't know the difference between democracy and public relations gimmicks and hasn't the decency to value the sensibilities of those rare places in America where people live that do—then a pox on it. There are eleventh and twelfth commandments in Vermont: "Thou shalt not use the name of town meeting in vain" and "Do not covet thy neighbor's democracy."

That did it! We decided to toss "the other forty-nine" out of the Union and become again a confederation of one. In short:

WE ARE OUTTA HERE!

Alfred Le Croix stopped and closed his notebook. Moisture glistened on his forehead. For an instant total silence hovered in the Old Stone House, broken only by the snap of the fire and the sound of snow falling on the windows. The Special Forces troopers stood transfixed. Then from the back of the room a single, naked clap was heard. Then another.

Bentley whirled with a deadly cut-the-crap stare, but it was too late. The Green Berets were applauding in earnest. Then Anthony Morehead stood up, tucked his notepad under his arm, and began to pound his hands together, nodding his head affirmatively. A Vermonter cheered and was immediately joined by a lusty, deep-throated chorus of support from the American soldiers. Everyone in the room followed Morehead's lead and leaped to their feet. Never in its long history had the Old Stone House come so close to shaking. "Atta boy, Alfred!" yelled Sallie Soule.

5

When It's Red in the Morning . . .

February 4, 1991
(TUGWOS Plus 8)
The Old Stone House
Brownington

Bentley Bentley shifted carefully in his chair. He didn't want to waken Jennifer Brown, who had fallen asleep soon after Le Croix's speech ended. It was 7:15, and the negotiations with the Vermont Republic were not going well.

"It's obvious," he said to the Revolutionary Council, "that you people have some legitimate concerns." To himself he said, *Fifteen minutes more from that old sodbuster, and I'd have lost the whole Special Forces task force. Thank God Tony Morehead is here.* But a quick glance around the room revealed that his favorite assistant was nowhere to be seen. So far, the nineteen Special Forces troopers had not budged. *Good.*

He continued with a condescending chuckle. "But you folks took us by surprise! Why couldn't you have given us a little warning first? If you'd only given us a hint of what was coming—a sign. At least we could have talked." This last was said with just a touch of reproachfulness.

"Sign!" snorted Sallie Soule, leaping to her feet. "Let me tell you about signs, sergeant. We Vermonters know all about them. Wild geese in the sky, a tinge in the sumac, a swelling in the cow's udder. You Americans, it seems, do not. Despite the billions spent on national security, it is most odd that no one in the White House caught on to the coming ouster of 'the other forty-nine.' We left signs everywhere. Any lame-brained FBI agent on a busman's holiday should have put them together."

She paused for a breath. "You want signs? I'll give you signs!" She fumbled through a stack of papers, grabbed one, and leaned toward Bentley Bentley. "Did you know, for instance, that for the last ten years more and more out-of-staters have been mistaken for deer during hunting season? It's right here in the *published* statistics! What did you want us to do, hit you over the head with it?" Soule paused triumphantly, and Bentley Bentley cast an anxious glance at a group of red-clad men standing in the back. "And there's more," continued Soule as she settled back to read.

Signs of Rebellion

- The price of maple syrup quadrupled between 1970 and 1990.
- Vermont high schools began to *require* Japanese, karate, international relations, and revolutionary theory. American history was made optional.[1]
- Still another power line was built from Canada through Vermont to Massachusetts, turning Vermont into a genuine "international power broker."
- A dramatic increase in the number of mysterious condominium fires was reported.
- More and more out-of-staters were mistaken for wild turkeys during hunting season.
- Someone painted a strategic "Un" on the "Welcome to Vermont" sign on I-91 at the Vermont-Massachusetts border.
- In 1989 and 1990 the percentage of Vermonters who failed to file income tax returns jumped dramatically.
- A shadowy character known as "the trail sign bandit"

[1] Vermont history became a requirement in all the state's colleges.

directed skiers off into gorges, over cliffs, and down dark trails into the deep forest, and they were never heard from again.

- Vermont completely restructured its ZIP Codes without asking anyone.
- The circulation of the Sunday *New York Times* began to fall dramatically while that of *Behind the Times, The Barton Chronicle, The Vanguard,* and *The Black River Tribune* rose sharply.
- Post offices began to fly the Vermont flag instead of the American flag, and Governor Sanders's picture appeared on the wall replacing President Haig's.
- Vermont lowered its drinking age back to eighteen and reset the speed limit on the interstate at fifty-five.
- High school sporting events began with a rendition of "Hail, Vermont" instead of "The Star-Spangled Banner."
- Howard Dean was seen signing up for a course in Vermont history at Johnson State College.
- At a public hearing on the nuclear dump question in 1985, a man leaped up from the bleachers of a packed high school auditorium, pointed at federal officials on the stage, and yelled, "Have you guys ever heard of Ethan Allen and the Green Mountain Boys?"
- Tent cities began to appear on U.S. National Forest lands.
- More and more out-of-staters were mistaken for ducks during hunting season.

Soule looked up at Bentley Bentley. "No," she said sharply as he opened his mouth, "you listen to *me*!

"With billions spent on intelligence over the past quarter-century, how could FUS have overlooked the revolutionary pamphleteering going on in Vermont? Were they so busy breaking into the offices of insignificant psychiatrists, pulling dirty tricks on the party out of office, and playing cloak-and-dagger that they failed to notice the obvious? You didn't *see* the 'Republic of Vermont' license plates traveling all over America on Vermont cars?

"How is it," she hurried on, "that FUS missed the inflammatory remark of Vermont's most famous senator, George Aiken, 'When you go to the White House, get a seat near the door, so that when they dim the lights, you can sneak out.' 'Sneak out'! There it is—secessionism! This remark was published by Vermont historian Charles Morrissey a full decade before TUGWOS!"

Soule was hot! She bored in. "With all that dough spent on intelligence gathering, how could you have missed the July 1971 issue of the Vermont magazine *Chittenden*? One Jay Madison wrote a piece entitled, 'VIM Can Mean Nationhood,' about the Vermont Independence Movement. In this article Sam Hand, a professor of history, argues that when the name 'Burlington Municipal Airport' was changed to 'Burlington International Airport,' it was due to behind-the-scenes actions of the VIM. Hand also shrewdly observed that it is not inconsequential that Vermont's largest insurance company is named *National* Life of Vermont, not *State* Life of Vermont."

"But Ms. Soule—" protested Bentley Bentley.

"That's *Mrs.* Soule to you, buddy!" snapped Soule. Bentley Bentley glanced helplessly at Madeline Harwood, who smiled sweetly.

Soule marched on. "In newspapers as widely circulated as *The Stowe Reporter* and *The Burlington Free Press,* economist David Hale of St. Johnsbury established the intellectual basis for the secession. Hale's primary work, the article 'The Republic of Vermont: A Modest Proposal,' appeared in the October 1973 issue of *The Stowe Reporter.* Published in broad daylight, it covered an array of ideas dear to all Vermont secessionists. Let me read you a few:

- Hale says, "If political ideas are contagious, the 201st anniversary of Vermont's founding as a Republic could also be the year in which Vermont becomes the first state in more than a century to sprout a full-fledged independence movement." Nothing hidden there. This courageous Vermonter published it right under the noses of the FBI and CIA. What'd they want us to do — send it by courier?

- Hale says, "In order to become dedicated separatists, all Vermonters must recognize the economic and geopolitical logic of creating North America's first microstate. Our two-hundred-year-old relationship with the United States has left us a relatively poor and insignificant province."

- "Imagine the Vermont capital of Montpelier," says Hale, "with 130 foreign embassies. . . . Indeed, in a few years Montpelier would probably boast one of the most unique combinations of rural and cosmopolitan lifestyles anywhere in the world — offering within the same short radius good fishing and hunting, snowmobile races, stock car derbies, the opera *La Bohème* and a cocktail party with the British Ambassador."

- But Hale is practical, too. "Independence would also permit us to deal with our long-festering welfare problems in traditional Vermont ways. In the good old days before reapportionment of the state legislature, the small towns of the Northeast Kingdom used to get people off the welfare list by electing them town representative. . . . The Republic could resurrect this practice by exporting its few lazy welfare recipients as ambassadors and diplomats. We could let them look after the embassy in Bulgaria, Paraguay, and other cheap-living countries where someone can be pensioned off at one-tenth the cost of supporting them here.

"These were all published?" Bentley asked hoarsely. "They're in *print*?"

"You betcha," said Soule, "and with this kind of secessionist comet in the heavens over Vermont, no one can ever say we were sneaky about what we've done. Understood?"

"Understood," said the lieutenant colonel, wishing Anthony Morehead would return. He was bothered, too, by the fact that the eleven Special Forces troopers in the corner had applauded Sallie Soule's remarks. It was now 7:45 P.M.

By 9:30, the negotiations were complete. Madeline Harwood, speaking for the Revolutionary Council, had held firm. Vermont would not accept "the other forty-nine" back into its fold. Bentley Bentley was given a copy of the Moscow Covenant to take back to Washington. When he protested that the Supreme Court would never accept it, Harwood said, "Your court can do whatever it wants with it. It can TUGWOS if it wants to." Soule chuckled.

"We know the President will be upset," said Madeline Harwood. "Perhaps if you remind him that he is *still in charge* of 'the other forty-nine,' he'll be happier. Besides"—she glanced at Jennifer Brown—"what was FUS going to do, nuke us?"

It was over. The Grange women were cleaning up the room. Bentley Bentley sought out one of Morehead's assistants (Morehead had not returned) and hissed into his ear, "We're getting nowhere with this. Start up the choppers. Let these hillbillies have their country for now. They'll screw it up soon enough, and we'll be ready when they do." He paused ominously. "Yes indeed, we'll be ready."

But at 9:35 a snow-covered chopper pilot pushed open the front door and hurried across the room toward Bentley Bentley. His face was whiter than the snow. Turning his boss toward the wall, he said tensely, "Morehead has defected."

Bentley Bentley's reaction was automatic. He was a trained military man. "Don't just stand there!" he cried. "Grab those three Green Berets over there and hunt the traitor down!" He paused and turned to look. "*Three* Green Berets? Oh m'god." Ashen, he turned back to his pilot, but there was no help there.

"The rest are gone, too," the pilot said. "They're over in Ketchner's barn. He's given them sanctuary, all fifty-three of them, plus Morehead and six of your staffers. There are only seventeen of us left out of the original seventy-four."

Bentley collapsed into a folding chair.

"And that's not all," said the pilot. "The choppers won't start."

"They won't *start*?" screamed Bentley, leaping to his feet.

"Frozen solid, sir."

"No matter," said a bright voice. Bentley Bentley whirled around to face a smiling Madeline Harwood. "We'll take care of it."

"What can you do?"

"We'll jump ya," said Sallie Soule with a grin.

6

The Vermont Republic's Declaration of Independence

February 6, 1991
(TUGWOS Plus 10)
Washington, D.C.

Dick Snelling was in a hurry. His appointment with President Haig was at 10:45, and traffic was clogged. Cars reminded him of roads, and roads reminded him that if Haig had not defeated Howard Baker in the Republican primary in 1988, he would have been named secretary of transportation by Baker, who, like Haig, could have easily defeated Teddy Kennedy, whom the Democrats had finally nominated for President. It was going to be interesting, thought the former Governor of Vermont, to drop this particular document on the President's desk.

He reached into his briefcase and took out a brown manila folder. In it was the new Vermont Declaration of Independence, preceded by edited notes from a subcommittee of the Revolutionary Council. From the cool comfort of his limousine, Snelling began to read.

Brownington, Vermont
February 3, 1991

As Keith Jennison pointed out in his book *Yup, Nope and Other Vermont Dialogues,* Vermont is a nation of tight talkers. Another Vermonter, Wolfgang Mieder, teaches this in his collection of Vermont proverbs entitled *Talk Less and Say More*. Thus, in thinking about a new Declaration of Independence for the Republic of Vermont, we tried to be brief and to the point. The U.S. Declaration of Independence contains 1,324 words — too many.

For example, the U.S. Declaration begins:

> When in the Course of human events, it becomes necessary for one people to dissolve the political bands which have connected them with another, and to assume among the Powers of the earth, the separate and equal station to which the Laws of Nature and of Nature's God entitle them, a decent respect to the opinions of mankind requires that they should declare the causes which impel them to the separation.

Vermonters might simply say, "WHEN YOU'RE GETTING THE SHAFT, IT'S BEST TO LEAVE AND TELL WHY."

Further on the national document reads,

> Prudence, indeed, will dictate that Governments long established should not be changed for light and transient causes; and accordingly all experience hath shown, that mankind are more disposed to suffer, while evils are sufferable, than to right themselves by abolishing the forms to which they are accustomed. But when a long train of abuses and usurpations, pursuing invariably the same Object evinces a design to reduce them under absolute Despotism, it is their right, it is their duty, to throw off such Government, and to provide new Guards for their future security. — Such has been the patient sufferance of these Colonies; and such is now the necessity which constrains them to alter their former Systems of Government.

Vermonters might say, "IT'S BROKE. WE'D BEST FIX IT."

Any number of to-the-point proclamations might serve as Vermont's new Declaration of Independence.

THE VERMONT REPUBLIC'S DECLARATION OF INDEPENDENCE

a. The One-Word Version
"Liberty"

b. The Two-Word Version
"Kiss Off"

c. The Three-Word Version
"Ripped. Leaving. 'Bye."

d. The Four-Word Version
"Dear Congress: *Shove it.*[1]"

e. The Five-Word Version
"We're going it alone. Out!"

f. The Two-Bit Version

"Remember the first flag? It read, 'Don't Tread on Me.' We told you we'd leave if you did, and you did, and we have."

g. The Long (Thirty-Seven-Word) Version

[1] Spelled, of course, TUGWOS.

"We're going up to view the pasture spring; we're going to stop and rake the leaves away (and wait to watch the water clear, we may): we'll be gone forever. — You could've come too. Now you can't."[2]

Actually, the Republic has chosen Vermont's original Declaration of Independence of 1777. It worked then and, with minor editing, it'll work now.[3]

In Convention of the representatives from the several counties and towns of the New Hampshire Grants, holden at Westminster, January 15, 1777, by adjournment.

Whereas the Honorable the Continental Congress did, on the 4th day of July last, declare the United Colonies in America to be free and independent of the crown of Great Britain; which declaration we most cordially acquiesce in: And whereas by the said declaration the arbitrary acts of the crown are null and void, in America, consequently the jurisdiction by said crown granted to New York government over the people of the New Hampshire Grants is totally dissolved:

We, therefore, the inhabitants, on said tract of land, are at present without law or government, and may be truly said to be in a state of nature; consequently a right remains to the people of said Grants to form a government best suited to secure their property, well being and happiness. We the delegates from the several counties and towns on said tract of land, bounded as follows: South on the North line of Massachusetts Bay; East on Connecticut River; North on Canada line; West as far as the New Hampshire Grants extends:

---

[2] From Robert Frost's "The Pasture." ("I'm going out to clean the pasture spring; I'll only stop to rake the leaves away (And wait to watch the water clear, I may): I shan't be gone long. — You come too.")

[3] We'd change "New Connecticut" to "Vermont," cut out references to the Congress — which were placed there just to humor it anyway — change a few dates, and rework the second paragraph to reflect our present dilemma. Otherwise, it's quite beautiful as it is.

After several adjournments for the purpose of forming ourselves into a distinct separate state, being assembled at Westminster, do make and publish the following Declaration, viz.:

That we will, at all times hereafter, consider ourselves as a free and independent state, capable of regulating our internal police, in all and every respect whatsoever — and that the people on said Grants have the sole and exclusive and inherent right of ruling and governing themselves in such manner and form as in their own wisdom they shall think proper, not inconsistent or repugnant to any resolve of the Honorable Continental Congress.

Furthermore, we declare by all the ties which are held sacred among men, that we will firmly stand by and support one another in this our declaration of a state, and in endeavoring as much as in us lies, to suppress all unlawful routs and disturbances whatever. Also we will endeavor to secure to every individual his life, peace and property against all unlawful invaders of the same.

Lastly we hereby declare, that we are at all times ready, in conjunction with our brethren in the United States of America, to do our full proportion in maintaining and supporting the just war against the tyrannical invasions of the ministerial fleets and fellow brethren, and with fire and sword to ravage our defenceless country.

The said state hereafter to be called by the name of NEW CONNECTICUT.

This, then, was the document Snelling was to deliver to President Haig, which he did. Later, as he was being ushered out of the Oval Office, his mission completed, Snelling overheard the President ask, "I understood everything except that final statement. What did he mean by the word *TUGWOS,* anyway?"

But Snelling did not hear Haig's next remark. "Look, I'm fed up with these hayseeds. The whole world is laughing at me. And when they are laughing at me, they are laughing at America! And when they are laughing at America, do you know who they are laughing at?" Haig turned expectantly to Jim Bakker, special assistant to the President for morality.

"They are laughing at God, Mr. President," said Bakker reverently.

Bentley Bentley, the only other man in the room, looked at the floor.

"Two more weeks! I'll give you two more weeks. If they haven't taken us back by then . . . Meanwhile," he continued, "a little flattery never hurts. It shouldn't be hard to sucker those hicks back into the fold."

President Haig then sat down and dictated the following telegram to Vermont:

February 6, 1991

The Revolutionary Council
The Republic of Vermont
Brownington, Vermont 081[4]

Dear Vermonters:

Lieutenant Colonel Bentley Bentley has reported to me on the conference at the Old Stone House. I have the Moscow Covenant and the other documents from the Brownington meeting, and I must say they are impressive. Moreover, Richard Snelling has just handed me a copy of your Declaration of Independence.

After due consideration, I have to admit that you are

---

[4] Vermont's new ZIP Codes number from 001 (Victory — the smallest town) to 246 (Burlington — the largest city). There is one number for each city or town in the Republic.

right. We are wrong. Please forgive us, and let us come back. Remember the words of your own poet laureate, Robert Frost, who said, "Home is the place that when you go there, they have to take you in."

We, the other forty-nine, have always thought of Vermont as our National Homeland. Without you, Thanksgiving is a hollow day, the sleigh bells of Christmas are silent, and autumn's colors fade to gray. We can't live without you. You were our conscience, our soul, the epitome of every good thing America has ever claimed for itself. Please — you have to take us in.

Sincerely,

President Alexander Haig

The Revolutionary Council of the Republic of Vermont sent the following telegram in reply:

Brownington, Vermont
February 8, 1991

Alexander Haig, President
The White House
Washington, FUS

Dear President Haig:

Get Lost, You Turkey!

Sincerely,

The Revolutionary Council
of the Republic of Vermont

7

The Nation Reacts

News of the Vermont rebellion spread like wildfire across the nation. Most Americans had to look at a map to find Vermont. Many were immediately seized by a cold grip on their hearts (like the time you ran away from home as a kid, came back, and were met at the door by your parents, who looked you straight in the eye and said, "It's too late. We don't want you here anymore"). It was almost as if the last chance to preserve America had been lost. It was like death. Vermont was simply not there anymore.

A kind of melancholy began to set in. Journalists reminded Americans of the words of historian Bernard de Voto—"There is no more Yankee than Polynesian in me, but when I go to Vermont I feel like I'm traveling toward my own place"—and of those of columnist Neal Pierce: "Vermont is perhaps the only place in America a stranger can feel homesick for before he has even left it."

But these were considered responses. Immediate reactions included:

Mikhail Gorbachev   "Is that the city that voted for the nuclear freeze?"

Admiral John C. Poindexter	"Have they taken hostages? I wonder if they need any missiles."
George Wallace	"Hot damn! It took them Yankee peckerwoods, but somebody finally done it."
Jimmy Carter	"My heart goes out to the families of the hostages at Killington."
Richard Nixon	"Pardon me?"
Bob Dole	"Who gets their electoral votes?"
Governor Mario Cuomo	"What's going to happen to the Rouses Point Bridge now?"
Sylvester Stallone	"Yoooooo Vermont!"
John Madden	"It's simple! Vermont's lined up here. The U.S. is there — then boom, boom. Mud, blood. I like it. And they're playing on real grass. Boy, that's the way to ring Uncle Sam's bell!"
Lieutenant Colonel Oliver North	"Were they following orders?"
Teddy Kennedy	"When do I say, *'Ich bin ein Vermonter'*?"

Nancy Reagan	"I don't see any need to wake him up. It's only one little state."
Bob Newhart	"We've got to get Darryl the hell out of there."
Henry Kissinger	"Ve cannot take this lightly. Their geo-political position is of great strategic relevance in the North American balance of power. I suggest pre-emptive strikes against their maple syrup reserves."
Governor John Sununu	"Good riddance!"
Gary Hart	"If they need a navy, I could sell them *Monkey Business*."
Phil Rizzuto	"Holy cow!"
John Naisbitt	"It's the eleventh megatrend! I knew it all along."

Chief Justice William Rehnquist	"Does this mean I'll need a visa to get to Greensboro? Will they let me sell my house to anyone I want to?"
Charles Kuralt	"There goes the best state in the Union to be 'on the road' in."
William F. Buckley, Jr.	"It's metaphysically absurd."
Yogi Berra	"Vermont ain't gone till it's gone."

Your Secessionist Aptitude

February 11, 1991
(TUGWOS Plus 15)
Montpelier, Vermont

The Tavern Motor Inn was abuzz with excitement. The legislature (which had not met since it had named the Revolutionary Council on the first day of TUGWOS) had dissolved itself and the RC at 10:30 that morning.[1] The day before, all power had been turned over to a Provisional Government stationed at Brownington, which would operate through a "Town Meeting of the Republic" format. Rumors bounced off the walls of Montpelier watering holes like hail off a tin roof: the Provisional Government would be moved to Northfield; President Haig had called still another meeting of the National Security Council; France had refused to recognize Vermont; Vermont's delegation to the UN had been refused passage through New York; the hostages at Killington were demanding wine with their meals; the newly formed Second Vermont Snowmobile Battalion had retaken Fort Ticonderoga in a bloodless daylight

---

[1] Several dozen members didn't get the message and for weeks to come could be found milling around the State House wondering why the door wouldn't open.

attack that very morning.[2] Another rumor had it that a Vermonter had pulled a Dartmouth professor from the Connecticut River after he, forgetting that Mares had blown up the Norwich to Hanover bridge, found himself momentarily airborne over the Connecticut. The citizens of Hanover were so moved, they were preparing to request admission to Vermont as its 247th town.

Former Speaker of the Vermont House Ralph Wrong was in a good mood as he sat with his morning coffee surrounded by a cluster of adoring legislators.

"Which one of you people would like to get me a paper?" He grinned.

Three lawmakers—two Democrats and a Republican—leaped to their feet, crying "Me, sir, please, me?"

"What about the rest of you?" said the former speaker playfully. "Want to end up on the Fish and Wildlife Committee?"

At that moment Michael Heartburn, former Republican House leader, appeared accompanied by absolutely no one. "Congratulations, Ralph," he said dourly.

"Oh, you know," said Wrong brightly; then, turning to his entourage, "Rumor has it the Provisional Government in Brownington has named me ambassador to the UN."

Leaping to his feet, Governor Vincent Illusory[3] snapped

---

[2] Like some of the other rumors, this one turned out to be true. It was the last act of open hostility in TUGWOS. When FUS did not retaliate, it was clear TUGWOS was over.

[3] Kunin was not re-elected because in September 1988 she was kidnapped by solid waste bandits and held incommunicado in a Northeast Kingdom landfill until after the election. She was released unharmed two months later. But meanwhile Burlington mayor Bernie Sanders swept to victory over Michael Heartburn. Sanders only lasted one term because he bullied the state Board of Education into de-certifying all elementary schools that failed to require the course "Giants of Socialist Thought." An angry electorate swung from left to right and chose Vincent Illusory governor in a landslide in 1990.

his suspenders and did his best Ed Norton imitation. "Atta boy, Ralph!"

"Thank you, Governor. Now why don't you run along and get my paper."

"Well, Wrong," said Heartburn, "maybe you won't be so happy after you've seen the paper." But secretly he knew that Ralph Wrong would make a hell of an ambassador to the UN. Sooner or later, the Soviet ambassador would be fetching his paper.

"Oh?" said Wrong, mildly interested.

"Yeah, if we're forced to take the test, they may banish us both."

"Test? What test?" asked Wrong, even more interested now. But Heartburn had walked away.

When Governor Illusory returned with the newspaper, Ralph Wrong got his answer. It was contained in an open letter right in the middle of the first page.

Residents
Republic of Vermont

Dear Fellow Secessionists:

Secession, like living through winter anywhere north of Boston, is serious business. Some talk about "getting even with Uncle Sam" while they fill out tax forms, but come April 15, they mail the forms and their checks and slink home to wait fearfully for an audit notice.

Others move away to France or Fiji or Florence and stay until the trust fund gives out. Still others march in an occasional protest (as long as the weather is cooperative). Some write letters to the editor, or to the President, or to their congressman. But precious few have the guts, toughness, and thick skull and skin needed for secession. We're talking hardball here.

Below is a test for would-be secessionists who may be heading for Vermont. We urge anyone whose juices are stirred by the romance of secession to take it before coming to Vermont. The exam will also work for Vermonters who may have doubts about their own capacity to live in the new Republic.

SECESSIONIST'S APTITUDE TEST

1. What year did the U.S. government impose the 55-mile-an-hour speed limit on Vermont?

2. In what state did Shays' Rebellion take place?

3. Ohio has been dumping acid rain on Vermont for nearly twenty years, trashing her lakes and forests.

What should Vermont's response be?

a. A resolution should be introduced in all town meetings protesting acid rain.
b. Vermont's congressman should introduce appropriate legislation to deal with it.
c. Vermonters should boycott Ohio products.
d. Vermont should banish Ohioans from Vermont, restrict their travel inside the state, refuse to sell any Vermont product in Ohio, and seed Lake Erie with piranha fish.
e. Vermont should arm missiles directed at Ohio smokestacks, triggered by acid rain gauges on Camel's Hump.[4]

4. When the federal government threatened to cut off highway funds from states that did not raise their drinking age to twenty-one, several states filed a lawsuit contesting the constitutionality of this act. Name two.

5. How often do you forget the words to "The Star-Spangled Banner"?

a. Never
b. Seldom
c. Often
d. The Star-Spangled what?

6. When you fill out your income tax forms, do you check the little box that donates a dollar to a fund to finance federal elections?

a. Yes
b. No

7. Which bumper sticker appeals to you most?

---

[4] Thus, Ohioans who bring acid rain down on Vermont will trigger their own fate. It will be out of Vermont's hands. If the gauge goes up, so do the rockets. Think about it.

a. "Have you hugged your kid today?"
b. "Secessionists do it for keeps."
c. "Question authority."
d. "Nuke the unborn gay whales."

8. Rank the following parts of the U.S. Constitution according to their odor.

PEEE-U

1. The Elastic Clause   a. _____
2. The Reserved Powers Clause   b. _____
3. The Supremacy Clause   c. _____
4. The Bill of Rights   d. _____

AHHHH

9. Which of the following states was the *last* to ratify the U.S. Constitution?

a. New York
b. Virginia
c. Rhode Island
d. New Hampshire

10. Rank the following quotes according to how much they appeal to you.

I REALLY LIKE IT

1. "Damn the torpedoes, full   a. _____
   speed ahead!"
   (Admiral Farragut)
2. "A hungry man is not   b. _____
   a free man."
   (Adlai Stevenson)
3. "The tree of liberty is fed   c. _____
   by the blood of patriots."
   (Thomas Paine)
4. "If I could save the Union   d. _____
   without freeing any slave,
   I would do it."
   (Abraham Lincoln)   *YUK*

11. Do you "fall back" in the fall and "spring forward" in the spring?

12. Have you ever laughed out loud at a presidential news conference?

13. Can you name twenty differences between Vermont and New Hampshire?

14. Do you favor the passage of a federal gun control law?

15. Should Vermont remain in the eastern time zone?

16. Do you support Vermont's current tax structure, which is "piggy-backed" on the federal schedule?

17. Do you still celebrate holidays on the day they fall, or do you go for the three-day weekend?

18. Should helmet laws be required for:
    a. Motorcyclists
    b. Skateboarders
    c. Automobile drivers
    d. Pedestrians
    e. Babies in carriages
    f. All of the above
    g. None of the above

19. Why did Shays rebel?

20. On June 7, 1987, the following story appeared in *The Burlington Free Press*. In a hundred words or less, explain what's going on.

    Sometimes it's difficult for Vermonters to understand some of the newcomers who are flocking to the Green Mountain State.
    Deane Willson, a farmer and chairman of

Waterford's Board of Selectmen, said he recently went to help a neighboring farmer with planting, and while they were working, he happened to see a young woman go jogging by.

"That one of your new neighbors?" he asked his friend. Yes, he was told, and a flatlander for sure.

It seems a few days earlier the man's two sons were out mending some fence along the roadside when she went jogging by. In an effort to be friendly, one of them suggested that if she needed the exercise, they had plenty of more productive things she could do than run back and forth along the road.

"That's the trouble with you farmers," the woman shot back. "You're just too lazy to jog!"

Answers

1. 1974
2. Massachusetts
3. d or e
4. South Dakota and Vermont are two of the eleven.
5. d
6. b
7. b or c
8. a–3, b–1, c–2, d–4
9. c
10. a–3, b–1, c–4, d–2
11. No. People ought to go by any damned time they see fit.
12. I can't remember one I didn't laugh at.
13. Yep.
14. Get serious.
15. No.
16. No.
17. Vermonters still use the one-day weekend.
18. g
19. He felt like it.
20. The essay question needs no explanation. If it does, you should banish yourself.

Where Do You Stand?

Percent Correct

0 to 30	*A Lost Cause:*	Go home, buy more life insurance, and enroll in a video club.
30 to 60	*There's Some Hope:*	Go home, read *Speaking from Vermont, Contrary Country,* and *Vermont: A History,* cancel all your life insurance, learn to use a chain-saw, and give us a call in two years.
60 to 80	*Apprentice Secessionist:*	You may come to Vermont provision-ally. Secessionist status will be awarded after you have earned your first five merit badges.*
80 to 100	*Secessionist Jedi:*	Welcome to the Green Mountain Federation!

* Merit badges may be earned in the following categories:
  - Draft-card burning
  - Sheep herding
  - Publishing in *Soldier of Fortune*
  - Sassing bureaucrats
  - Wood-fire generators
  - Tourist put-ons or put-downs
  - Agriweapons
  - Foreign policy
  - Bluff
  - Alternative agriculture

Ralph Wrong finished reading and leaned back in his chair, satisfied. Piece of cake, he thought. Some of the questions were so easy. How do you tell Vermont from New Hampshire? Hell, when you're facing north, New Hampshire's the one on the right of the river.

A Secessionist Jedi
Ralph Nading Hill

In his book *Contrary Country*, 1950, he begins:

Tremors Under the Timberline

When Doomsday comes, perhaps countries and states, as well as men, will stand before the bar of judgment. If this occurs, it will be entertaining to know what disposition is made of Vermont, the state conceived in controversy between New Hampshire and New York, and reared in rebellion.

Fires of rebellion, which flamed for a hundred years, have not gone out. Coals of protest still smolder in town meetings, under the dome of the state capitol and in phrases spoken by Vermont legislators in Washington. Visitors to the Green Mountains find Vermonters chemically unable to endorse the popular view on any subject from politics to the weather. . . .

Rebellion runs through the entire fabric of the lives of this resistant people whose ancestors first came to till a resistant soil.

Two hundred and ninety pages later he ends it:

Epilogue

Certainly the ancestors of these people were wayward. Rebellion is their birthright. Then there is the land. There is a surprise in every turning of the various landscape of Vermont — a mellow field, a dark woods, a merry lake, a somber gorge, a bold mountain. And so it is with the people. Perhaps the strength of the hills is theirs also.

Conceived in controversy, fires of rebellion, coals of protest, smolder, wayward, rebellion as a *birthright* — these are secessionists' words. And finally, *surprise.* Yes, indeed. Surprise, Uncle Sam. We're gone.

9

The First Act of the New Republic

February 16, 1991
(TUGWOS Plus 20)
Brownington, Vermont

When the legislature dissolved the Revolutionary Council and created the Provisional Government on February 11, it suggested that the PG serve until July 4, 1991, when elections would be held for a totally new government. In honor of the success of the Brownington Summit, in which the Revolutionary Council successfully faced off against representatives of FUS, the Provisional Government established its headquarters in the Old Stone House, still the most secure building in Vermont. Madeline Harwood and Sallie Soule were kept on in the leadership posts but were now called co-moderators, since the new Provisional Government operated as a town meeting: that is, any Vermonter who wished to could show up and vote. Other moderators would be selected as the need arose. Ralph Wrong was named interim ambassador to the United Nations, and Dick Snelling became interim secretary of state. Both faced election in July.

At 3:45 P.M. on February 16, the Provisional Government issued its first proclamation:

Be it known that in open meetings assembled the People of Vermont have adopted (by a vote of 127 yups to 36 nopes) the following law: The new national language of Vermont will consist of one word.[1]

TUGWOS
(THE ULTIMATE GREAT WAR
OF SECESSION)

The word TUGWOS will be forever pronounced *shoveit* in English and will constitute Vermont's national vocabulary. The secondary language, English, will be used for everyday discourse if and until the occasion arises when the official national language is needed.

The new law's intent was further described in the proclamation.

Examples of what Vermonters might say when they feel the need to slip into their national tongue are:

- "You say you don't appreciate my hogs in your garden? Why don't you take one and TUGWOS."
- "Take this job and TUGWOS."
- "Listen, FUS, how we conduct negotiations with Finland is our own business, and if you don't approve, why don't you TUGWOS."
- "Look, twenty-five miles per hour is fast enough. Why don't you take your horn and TUGWOS."

[1] Meaning, of course, that Vermont's new unabridged dictionary was very small.

10

Crisis in Enosburg

February 20, 1991
(TUGWOS Plus 24)
Enosburg, Vermont

It had to come sooner or later—the first great crisis.
Would President Haig go bananas when he got the in-
famous "Turkey Note" and send the full force of FUS's
military might against Vermont? Would seed for the spring
planting fall under the new embargo FUS was threatening?
What if the government in Brownington collapsed? Worst
of all, what if it was a bad year for maple syrup and the
Republic lost its chance to start off on a sound financial
footing?

But no one could have predicted what happened in Enosburg on February 20, 1991, at 7:28 P.M.

The occasion was the final basketball game of the season
between Enosburg Falls and Richford. Little schools in
little towns, these archenemies packed the Enosburg gym.
The atmosphere was hot, sweaty. Cheerleaders from both
schools made spirited appearances. The teams were introduced to the crowd; the league championship and a trip to
the state finals were at stake.

Mal Boright prepared to call the action over WDEV in
Waterbury. The two referees walked to the center of the
floor, and a hush fell as the crowd waited for the needle to
be placed on the scratchy but still serviceable record of the
national anthem. The audience rose.

Then it happened.

Nothing.

Vermont *had* no national anthem. The principal of Enosburg High refused to start the game until one was played. Chaos broke loose.

"Play the old one!" someone hollered from the crowd.

"Never, you Tory sapsucker!" screamed an old lady.

"I've never seen anything like this!" gasped Boright. "There is chaos everywhere. Both coaches have called their teams back to the huddle, but they're having trouble keeping their attention. Several fights have broken out in the stands already. Wait! Some people are singing the American national anthem. Now they're being drowned out by stomping and yelling from the bleachers. The superintendent's wife is trying to sing 'Moonlight in Vermont' without music. But she's forgotten the words, and they're hooting her off the floor. 'It's sycamore, not hemlock, you idiot!' someone has yelled from the audience. Let's go to a commercial message from Manosh-Bigosh of Morrisville."

Then a strange thing happened. An old man stumbled out of the audience from the Richford side and walked slowly to center court. With pandemonium all around him threatening to bring Vermont to its knees, he took the mike and raised his hand to quiet the crowd. Miraculously the people fell silent. Then, in a voice heavy with his French-Canadian heritage, he began to sing:

> Oh, I wish I were in the land of syrup
> People there still answer "ayup"

Lookin' home
Lookin' home
Lookin' home, Yankee land.

It was as if an electric shock had passed through the crowd, riveting them to their seats, their eyes on the old farmer, their breath suppressed in their lungs. The old man continued, slowly, beautifully:

In Yankee land where I was born
Among the rocks that killed the corn
Lookin' home
Lookin' home
Lookin' home, Yankee land.

Oh, we'll always stay in *Ver*mont, ayup, ayup.
Though pickin's slim
We'll raise our kin
To "yup" and "nope" in *Ver*mont.

Ayup
Ayup
We'll raise our kin in *Ver*mont.

Ayup
Ayup
We'll raise our kin in *Ver*mont.

The old man stopped singing.

The audience, momentarily stunned, suddenly broke into a frenzy of wild cheering. Many started singing themselves, "Oh, I wish I were in the land of syrup . . ." The old man disappeared into the crowd, never to be seen again.

Two weeks later the Provisional Government, by a vote of 226 to 16, named "Yankee" the Vermont national anthem. It also voted a resolution of thanks to the mysterious old Vermonter from Richford who saved the Republic.

11

Now Whatta We Do?

February 24, 1991
(TUGWOS Plus 28)
Brownington, Vermont

It was actually hot on the south side of the Old Stone House in Brownington on the afternoon of February 24. The sun poured through the windows. Among the Vermonters who had come from all over the Republic that day, the mood was good. It promised to be clear that night and warmer on the morrow—a perfect sugar day. Perhaps God was sending an early run as a birthday present for the new nation. Chester Wheeler of Marlboro said his neighbor had tapped out the day before. Bill Mares and Frank Bryan stood in the rear. They alone for some reason seemed worried.

The first week for the Provisional Government in Brownington had been a busy one. In many ways it found itself in precisely the same position in which Vermont had found itself in 1777, the year the first Republic was born—in a "state of nature." Yet there were differences. For instance, the new Republic had to decide what to do with the junk that had accumulated over the previous two centuries.

During the first week the Provisional Government did the following:

- It nationalized former FUS National Guard armories into roller-skating rinks.

- It designated the Amtrak railroad bed the globe's longest bike path for the summer months and a cross-country ski trail for the winter.
- It further designated the railroad bed a "stand" for foreign deer hunters. For exorbitant fees, Fish and Wildlife employees would herd the deer out of the forest and up onto the old track bed.
- It reallocated lift lines at some ski resorts for use as great clotheslines for Vermont's wash. Base lodges were converted to laundromats equipped with washers, to be used by Vermont citizens free of charge. Vermont decided to take energy conservation seriously. Indoor clothes dryers were outlawed throughout the state.

- It ordered the boulders on Burlington's Church Street Marketplace[1] removed to one of Vermont's new national

[1] For two hundred years Vermonters had broken their backs picking stone off their fields. When Burlington decided to remove cars from its main street, it went out and found some of the biggest boulders in the state and dumped them in the middle of the road. Vermont is covered with rocks. Do we need them in the center of the state's largest city, too? We know city folks think it's chic to look country. But what will come next—little piles of cow manure interspaced with barbed wire and a planted tractor or two?

parks, the "Any Damned Fool Knows Better'n That" Park planned for Randolph. There they would be featured as a quintessential flatlander *faux pas* along with such things as old Sea Shell City signs, racing forms from the defunct horse-racing track in Pownal, and chunks of I-91 taken from north of St. Jay.

* It named Norm Runnion, editor of *The Brattleboro Reformer,* the director and principal editorial writer of Radio Free Vermont, which would beam outrageous broadsides over the eastern seaboard from atop Ascutney Mountain. His job was to make Vermont seem as unattractive as possible to developers but very, very attractive to homesteaders. Runnion was Vermont's most talented "stick it in your ear" editor. He once compared Bernie Sanders to Richard Nixon in a *Reformer* editorial.

The major decision of the second week, however, concerned the interstate highway system. It had to go. It symbolized all that the new Vermont found disgusting: speed, fumes, asphalt, flashing blue lights, and those goddamned ugly little fake green fenceposts between Bolton and Waterbury that wave in the wind to deflect dueling headlights. The feds built it for driving at 75 miles per hour just before they told us we could only go 55, after which they decided 65 was okay. Nice piece of work, guys. It passed Congress as a *defense* highway. What were they expecting—an invasion from Canada, or Russian troops pouring in from over the Arctic ice cap?

Enough. There was no reason for the interstate to go through an independent Vermont. The Provisional Government proclaimed that visitors would simply have to travel at Vermont's own pace again. If they were just passing through, they could easily pass around. Besides, no one seemed to be using the interstate anymore anyway except for crazed Canadians, eighteen-wheeler truck jockeys in various states of repose, and out-of-state tourists wondering where Vermont had gone to.

Besides, argued the PG, Rutland and Bennington counties

had suffered from highway envy for too long.[2] They'd always wished they had bigger ones. If the interstate were destroyed altogether, then everyone's would be the same size.

The PG suggested the interstate highway system could be:

- Chopped up into many little highways that lead nowhere.
- Divided into thousands of horseshoe pits to support the new nation's official sport.
- Preserved to become the site of a new international road race — the Vermont 400.[3]
- Converted into hundreds of summer bowling alleys and winter curling rinks.
- Used for snowmobile races (the northbound lane) and cross-country skiing (the southbound lane).
- Mined, and the materials — gravel and roadfill — sold to neighboring states.

The crisis was resolved, by 216 yups to 18 nopes, that the interstate would be sold by the mile to avant-garde artists. On it they would paint giant planetary murals that could be seen from aircraft, balloons, helicopters, and UFOs. Helicopter rides to view the paintings would profit the Republic's treasury year round.

Throughout the first two weeks a flood of specific public policy proposals poured into the headquarters of the Provisional Government from prominent Vermonters. Dick

[2] Bennington has a short piece of four-lane that starts nowhere and ends nowhere but succeeds in cutting a hole through some damned pretty country.

[3] The race would extend down one lane from Canada to Massachusetts, across the "No U-Turn" sign at the border, then back to Canada. To add the variety and danger needed to entice worldwide audiences, manure spreaders would be backed blindly onto the highway at random times during the race. Slow-moving school buses, joggers, and a Sunday driver or two would suddenly appear. Dead animals would also be tossed strategically onto the road and monitored by judges. Any car hitting one would be disqualified.

Snelling called and suggested that since he was the brightest person in Vermont, he should be named prime minister.[4] Peter Welch wrote to request that Howard Dean, Jim Guest, and Paul Poirier be banished to Butte, Montana.

John McClaughry suggested a great national debate between himself and Dick Snelling to see who the smartest person in Vermont really was. Bill Mares requested that half the streams in Vermont be declared "Fly Fishing Only." Vermont political analyst Vincent Naramore called for the Bennington Battle Monument to be moved to Hubbardton, since the battle of Bennington took place in New York but the Hubbardton battle took place in Vermont. He swore he wasn't biased because he was from Hubbardton.

Al Moulton asked that the area between the Winooski River and Route 4 be given to him for a development called Leachy Lake. Livingston Corporation of Hancock called to ask permission to use dried, deodorized human feces to make bricks for a new condominium development.[5] The Vermont Natural Resources Council proposed that the Pidgeon Mountain Corporation be nationalized. The Vermont Hog Butchers Association suggested that Orville Torpey of Pownal be included in the McClaughry-Snelling debate since he is smarter than either. Other requests were as follows:

Requestor	*Request*
The University of Vermont	Requested that tuition be raised to $178,000 for foreign students.[6]
Steve Morse	Asked to be included in the Snelling-McClaughry-Torpey debate.

[4] He was told that there would be no prime minister but that if there were, the position would go to Scudder Parker.

[5] To be known as Kaopectate Condos.

[6] They used to be called "out-of-state" students.

Peter Smith	Proposed that all Vermonters should be required by law to believe that he is a self-made man.
James Guest	Pleaded for any important national post that allowed him to stay home and take care of the kids.
Patrick Leahy	Requested that he be given the title "Patrick the Pious" and that his picture be placed in every classroom in the Republic over the inscription, EVERYTHING I SAY IS TRUE.
Maida Townshend	Demanded that all teachers' salaries be quadrupled immediately.[7]
Ben and Jerry	Requested a trade policy to keep Häagen-Dazs out of the freezer cases of the nation's stores.
The Cabot Creamery	Asked for a resolution forgiving them for selling "real Vermont butter" that had been purchased in the Midwest.

Because of the onslaught of suggestions, and because the Provisional Government wished to emphasize the democratic character of the new Republic at the outset, the following proclamation was issued:

[7] Townshend, the head of Vermont's powerful teachers' union, submitted the only request that carried a threat: "Or I'll call a national teachers' strike." The Provisional Government sent the following telegram to Ms. Townshend from Brownington: DREAM ON, MAIDA.

Hear ye! Hear ye! The Vermont Republic issues its first annual "God for a Day" contest. Anyone who wishes to be ruler of Vermont for one day need only write a two-hundred-word essay entitled, "What I Would Do If I Ruled Vermont."

Below are some of the suggestions that were found in the over 1,248 essays that were received by the end of the week.

- Daylight Savings Time should be rejected forever.
- Vermont should sign a nonaggression pact with Finland.
- Water should be declared the national beverage.
- If Bernard Sanders ever uses the word *outrageous* again, he should be hunted down and forced to wear a tie whenever he is before the public—which, it seems, is always.
- Fast-food establishments should be prohibited from training new employees during rush hour.[8]
- April should be outlawed.
- The garage sale should be named the Vermont national pastime.
- The Craftsbury Fiddlers' Contest should be moved from Hardwick back to Craftsbury.
- Route 9 between Bennington and Brattleboro should be converted to the world's largest roller derby rink. Get from one end to the other alive, and you win.
- The next person, corporation, or state agency that suggested disturbing one pebble, one blade of grass, or one ounce of moss on the Long Trail for *whatever* reason under the sun, should be likewise hunted down and dunked in the nearest manure pit.
- Larry Bird should be given honorary Vermont citizenship.[9]

[8] The only reason we eat that junk is because it's fast. The random probability of encountering a new trainee on any given trip to a McDonald's or a Burger King must be at least fifty-fifty. We *know* what you're serving us—the least you can do is get it over with quickly!

[9] He's been called a white superstar in a black sport. He's more. He's a hick superstar in a city-slicker sport.

- No decision of the Republic of Vermont on any subject whatsoever should stand unless approved by Lola Aiken.
- Any driver who has to wait for a jogger trotting through traffic should receive a cash payment for their time from the government. We like joggers, but . . .
- The "mailbox game" should be made an official Vermont sport for teenagers, with the proviso that it be limited to old FUS mailboxes.
- A seatbelt law should be passed and strictly enforced. There should be no exceptions (except for any Vermonters who feel that saving their own ass is their own damned business). All those fastening their seatbelts because of this law would be given the following bumper sticker to place proudly on their car: I HAVE THE MENTALITY OF A CHILD. I NEED TO BE TOLD.
- A new source of energy for Vermont should be developed by harnessing the mouths of Peter Smith and Bernie Sanders.
- Anyone even suggesting that Vermont create a substitute for the tristate lottery lost during TUGWOS should get the liqua-store treatment, SS (sans snorkel).

The Provisional Government agreed to take all these suggestions into consideration and thanked Vermonters for their enthusiastic response. Final action was taken on the following items:

- The Ethan Allen Homestead was given the attention it deserves by making it the Mount Vernon of Vermont. George Washington's home overlooked the Potomac; Ethan's overlooked the Winooski. Both should be national shrines.
- To prepare for the greatest ETV auction ever, all federal property held in Vermont was confiscated. This act was known as "the Whole Nerd Buy Out."
- A law was passed stating that female deer had a right to attack joggers anytime they saw fit.
- A decision was made to allow the paving of no Vermont

road unless the majority of the residents living alongside it approved.

As the sun went down on the last day of the second full week of the PG's deliberations, its business seemed to be winding down. Decisions on what to do with the following items were tabled:

- The Volvo Tennis Tournament at Stratton
- Dennis Delaney
- Basketville
- The Barre-Montpelier Road
- The gentrification of Hardwick
- Alpine slides
- Harvey Carter

"Do I hear a motion for adjournment?" asked Scudder Parker, who had been elected Moderator for the Day, following the tradition set in place by Madeline Harwood and Sallie Soule at the PG's first meeting. Parker was a good moderator since he could also offer the opening prayer.

"Mr. Moderator!" yelled Bill Mares as the noise of adjournment began to rise. "Mr. Moderator, before we adjourn, I am afraid I bring worrisome news that demands our immediate attention."

Silence fell and heads turned, recognizing the legendary Mares, the hero of the Hanover Bridge caper and, many suspected, the man who had singlehandedly slashed the tires on the seven F-111 U.S. Air Force jets parked at Burlington International Airport the night before TUGWOS.

Mares headed for the front of the room.

"Bill!" hissed Frank Bryan.

Mares turned back. "What?" he whispered. "Did I forget my notes?"

"Only flatlanders walk to the front of the hall. Do it from here, Bill! Geesum!"

What Bill Mares had to say that day would have been bad news coming from anywhere in the hall. To the suddenly hushed and somber crowd, he said, "I have it on good authority that General—I mean President Haig is planning a raid on this very building on Tuesday morning at ten-thirty." Mares raised his hand to quiet the crowd. "They know how to get here, and they know the layout of the building. Remember, our first meeting with Bentley Bentley was in this very room."

A former Special Forces trooper, now an employee at the Paltry Paving Company of Williston, yelled, "Let 'em come! I've still got my M-16!" Thunderous agreement followed.

Madeline Harwood leaped to her feet. "No! Young man, there will be no violence. Right, Sallie?"

"Well—"

"There, that's settled. Now Billy, what do they intend to do?"

"They intend to hit this place with a twenty-five-copter task force, capture the entire meeting, and fly us out of here to Washington as prisoners of war!"

Gasp!

"Whatta we do about it, Bill?" yelled Mary Picher, a truck driver who had driven up from Dorset for the meeting.

"My suggestion is that we take a couple hundred of the hostages (ones that refused to be ransomed anyway) from Killington and bring them up here Tuesday morning. The troops from FUS will pounce on them and whisk them away in no time. And," said Mares, "we won't have to feed them anymore."

"But won't Bentley Bentley and his gang know that they are out-of-state hostages and not real Vermonters at a town meeting?" asked Mrs. Harwood.

"Not if we tell the hostages that they are being sent to role-play a town meeting as part of Killington's regular excursion package for flatlanders," answered Mares. "We'll dress 'em up in bib overalls, straw hats, and boots. We'll teach 'em to say yup and nope. They'll love it."

"Genius!" exclaimed Soule. "Only flatlanders would mistake other flatlanders dressed up as real Vermonters for really real Vermonters. Hell, they'll be halfway to Washington before Bentley Bentley catches on."

"But where will we meet next week?" asked Chester Lima of Peru.

"How about the Old Meeting House in Newfane?" suggested Norm Runnion, who attended all sessions of the Provisional Government in his capacity as director of Radio Free Vermont.

"Done," said Harwood. "Now, do I hear a motion to adjourn? For those who have to milk and have come a long way, it's late!"

"Just one more question." Betsy Holland, a sixteen-year-old from North Country Union High School, was nervous but she spoke up. "Why are they still after us? I thought TUGWOS was over."

This time Mares did walk to the front of the room and Bryan let him.

"Yes, Betsy," said Mares, "TUGWOS is over. Yet FUS is not to be trusted. They've laid off us for a while, and every day that we survive, our international position is stronger. But"—his voice grew quiet and tense—"whether or not TUGWOS is ultimately successful will depend on our constant vigilance."

On that note the meeting ended.

12

Yups and Nopes

Town Meeting Day, 1991

It was no ordinary Town Meeting Day, the first spring Vermont faced the world as the planet's newest nation. The state government had atrophied after TUGWOS, the legislature dissolved, the courts abandoned. Governor Illusory had gone ice fishing. With the Provisional Government working overtime to keep the new Republic alive, all day-to-day governmental decisions reverted to their rightful position in the towns, which remained solid and steadfast. In matters political Vermont had returned to its roots! This situation worked so well that the Provisional Government, meeting in Newfane, decided that Vermont should start the process of rebuilding its government from the bottom up.

Accordingly, local government was the *only* article on the Warnings of Vermont town meetings in 1991. By late Tuesday evening a miraculous consensus had emerged from over 200 disparate meetings on Vermont's new democracy.

Wednesday morning the Provisional Government met and approved a document reflecting this consensus. It was agreed that the Provisional Government would continue to conduct the Republic's affairs for now. In the long term all power would be returned to the towns and cities except for a handful of powers given to the national legislature. It would retain the authority to decide, for instance, if the Republican or the cougar should be placed on the nation's endangered species list. The guiding principle of Vermont's new system was "variety is the spice of life."

If, for example, some towns wanted to have the less fortunate to work on community-service projects for their keep, they could. If others wanted to send them to Harvard and buy them Cadillacs, that was okay, too. Towns could make the rich swap places with the poor on an alternating-year basis. They could make the *wealthy* work on community-service projects. "All for one, one for all." It used to work in Vermont; it might again. Who'd know if it weren't tried?

Tax Volvos. Tax Arabian horses and polo ponies. Tax dogs that weighed under five pounds. Tax snowmobiles. Tax taxes. Let a hundred flowers bloom. Hell, let a thousand bloom! A little good ol' Vermont democracy never hurt anybody.[1] If it was ever suggested that a town or city not be allowed to do something, the correct response should be "Why the hell not?" As in:

- If Burlington wanted to own its own cable TV network, why the hell not?
- If Woodstock wanted to establish a local income tax to raise money, why shouldn't it?
- If Newport decided to dissolve itself into six ethnic villages, if Troy and Coventry decided to merge, if Brownington wanted to junk its town meeting and

---

[1] Except those who had it coming anyway.

declare itself the smallest city in the Northeast Kingdom, who'd say no?

- If Swanton passed an ordinance proclaiming yellow and purple the only colors of housepaint allowable inside the town, that was their business.
- If Wilmington wanted to eliminate taxes and finance all town services with coin drops, that was their affair, wasn't it?[2]
- Who was to say Hardwick couldn't insist that its schoolchildren wear uniforms or its town meeting be in July or canoe races be held down Main Street in April? This wasn't Russia.
- What was wrong with Stowe and Shelburne and Peru closing school in December and opening it up again in May? It's a free country, baby!
- If Townshend wanted to select its selectmen for life, let 'em. It was their town.
- If Chelsea considered it appropriate to charge a toll to get through town on Tunbridge Fair week, Vermonters could grin and bear it. It might be fun—add a little variety to the trip to the Fair. If the tolls got out of hand, we'd just carry machetes in the front seat.
- If Kirby wanted to make it a felony to be Scudder Parker or wanted to banish John McClaughry to Concord, they had the right in the Republic of Vermont.
- If White River Junction wanted to hold trustees' meetings in the Polka Dot Diner and their village meeting in the Coolidge Hotel, *why the hell not?*

By day's end it was agreed that only the towns could officially declare war. If war threatened, the selectmen of each town would convene at the national capital. If by a vote of at least twenty to one they declared that a state of war existed, then one would—with the following qualifications:

---

[2] Think what a haul they could make in leaf peeper season! Larry, Darryl, and Darryl out on the highway with twelve-gauge shotguns, leaning strategically against a couple of trash cans to toss money into, with a sign that read, COUGH UP A COIN FOR KINDERGARTEN.

- Immediately after a war was declared, the selectmen so voting would be drafted into the armed services as privates and sent to boot camp in Lunenburg.
- War would never be declared on Maryland, Idaho, Portugal, Finland, or Mozambique.
- The first target of any war with any nation anywhere would be Manchester, New Hampshire.
- If any nation ever declared war on FUS, Vermont would go to its defense. They're still family.

Other powers the towns retained were:

- The towns and cities could not coin money but they were the only governments that could spend it.
- The towns could establish their own codes of criminal justice.
- Only the towns could establish laws concerning education, welfare, and health and human services generally.
- The towns and cities could establish the office of Litter Warden, a roving constable with a green light on his car who could arrest, try, and punish anyone suspected of despoiling the countryside.[3]
- The towns could establish new town officers as they saw fit: a Tourist Assessor to check on the usefulness of certain tourists and a Barter Reeve to resolve disputes between citizens engaged in Vermont's principal method of economic exchange are examples. So are Condo Viewer, Overseer of the Rich, and Trail Commissioner.

In short, a town was pretty much free to govern itself. But it always had to use clear language. A model was provided by the citizens of a small town in Franklin County. Well into the 1940s, the good people of this town still elected a town officer, Killer of Dogs. Now, that's honesty in government!

It was late when the headlights began to wind into the hills of Vermont toward home very late on that first Town

[3] Such a law was introduced in the General Assembly of the old State of Vermont by John McClaughry but was unwisely defeated.

Meeting day after TUGWOS. Mud season was beginning, and no one hurried. Besides, they were exhausted after ten or twelve hours of straight politicking. But they were happy, too. TUGWOS had forced Vermont to return to its roots, its democracy. The people had challenged themselves to once again accept full responsibility for their own affairs. They had taken a sword as great as Ethan Allen's, and in one mighty slash they had cut away the underbrush of distant, deceitful, devious, dishonest government. They had tasted once again the joy of personal and communal liberty. For them it was a sweet season, as it was for the maple trees they passed on the darkened roadsides. The taste was good.

13

What'll You Take?
What'll You Give?

March 16, 1991
(TUGWOS Plus 48)
Somewhere South of the West River

Norm Runnion, director of Radio Free Vermont, stepped into a tiny studio somewhere in Windham County. He handed a sheaf of copy to Barre Jack, who had recently been hired as chief announcer. "And remember, Barre," he said, "no ad libs, and no advertisements for trips to Ireland."

"Got it," said Jack.

Moments later, one of the Republic's most critical broadcasts snapped out from the tower on Ascutney Mountain. All over Vermont, in garages, in pickup trucks, in the offices of the Rock of Ages Corporation, in kitchens big and small, in milking parlors, in hospitals and barbershops and warehouses—everywhere there was a radio—people listened to Radio Free Vermont.

But the broadcast found its way into other places, too. For WFREE[1] was being monitored around the world, at

---

[1] When WFREE first hit the airwaves, the FCC reacted angrily. Runnion's editorial reply the next day began: "The Federal Communications Commission of FUS has told us we must reduce our call letters from five to four to meet federal standards. They seem to have forgotten Vermont is a FREE country now! How's that for a four-letter word? Oh, by the way, FCC, why don't you take your four-letter rule and TUGWOS."

the Kremlin, in Beijing, in Paris, in Ottawa, and in Tokyo. No one, however, was more interested than Lieutenant Colonel Bentley Bentley, newly named director of President Haig's National Security Council; the NSC monitored WFREE from the White House. Bentley Bentley had given a standing order from his office in the basement:

"Tape everything! But when that goddamned country music stops and they begin to talk, triple tape it. Wherever I am, go get me!"

Bentley Bentley had put a cot in the Situation Room, resigned from his health club, divorced his wife, and had his meals brought to him. There was only one way to live down the embarrassment of the abortive raid on that awful Old Stone House when he and his men had "captured" a fake government made up of hostages that didn't want to be rescued.[2] That was to beat Vermont to the punch. He had to get into their *minds*.

So Bentley Bentley began to live and breathe Vermont. In two weeks he'd read every book he could find on the

---

[2] Bentley didn't catch on to the ruse until after he'd landed the copter fleet on the Capitol grounds in Washington in a grandstand demonstration of his success in capturing an entire foreign government. The hostages jumped to the ground, realized where they were, and began wailing and howling. "We're innocent flatlanders and we want to go back to Vermont!" they cried.

subject. But the more he read, the more jumpy he became. On March 15, soon after finishing Hill's *Contrary Country,* he had ordered his assistant, Robert McNearland, to bring in a special team of cryptographers to break Vermont's code.

"What code?" McNearland asked.

"The country music code, you idiot!" yelled Bentley Bentley.

"Oh."

"That's how they *communicate.* What else could those lyrics mean? A week ago they played the following songs in a row. . . . Wait." Bentley Bentley grabbed a yellow pad from atop the footlocker beside his cot. "Get *this,* McNearland."

"Okie from Muskogee"
"Little Green Apples"
"I'm Just an Old Chunk of Coal"
"Sunday Morning Comin' Down"

"And do you know what happened? I'll *tell* you what happened. The very next day, a Sunday, McNearland, those hillbillies made a coal-for-apples deal with a company in Oklahoma City!" He paused for effect. "Now, bring those crypto boys in here and get to work. Spare no expense!"

Christ, thought McNearland, an old C&W fan. He hoped they never played "Make the World Go Away." Bentley might be apt to nuke 'em before they tried.

The day after that conversation, March 16, the critical broadcast written by Norm Runnion and read by Barre Jack found its way into the basement of the White House and into the attentive ears of Bentley Bentley.

WE INTERRUPT OUR SCHEDULED BROADCAST OF THE ALBUM RICKY SCAGGS ... LIVE FROM TUSCALOOSA TO BRING YOU A RADIO FREE VERMONT EDITORIAL, FOLLOWED BY A SPECIAL ANNOUNCEMENT CONCERNING

THE REPORT RELEASED YESTERDAY BY THE NEWLY
CREATED GREEN MOUNTAIN COUNCIL OF ECONOMIC
ADVISERS. FIRST THE EDITORIAL.

Vermonters have always lived on the edge. When we tossed
out "the other forty-nine," we made the edge even sharper.
But no one said it would be easy, and Vermont has a long
tradition of making do. Our capacity to squeeze the last bit
of advantage from an unforgiving land comes clear in this
true story told by John Swainbank of St. Johnsbury.

Two Vermonters (a newcomer and a native) were gathering sap when they come upon a full bucket with a dead
mouse floating in it.

"I suppose you real Vermonters just pick out the mouse
and pour the sap into the tank anyway," said the newcomer.

"Nope," said the native, "a real Vermonter would squeeze
out the mouse first and then pour the sap into the tank."

That's living on the edge.
Freedom is not cheap; few good things are. Liberty costs.
It is not some flea market collectable. Which means that
Vermont has to learn again about doing without. As Vermont prepares to meet boycotts, retaliatory trade embar-
goes, sanctions, confiscatory tariffs, quotas, the lot, they
must reenter the school of self-reliance.

It hasn't taken us long to realize that we have to do without our double-stamp days, Pampers, freeze-dried foods,
floral telegrams, cheap gas, disposable razors, home videos,
commuter flights to Boston, microwave popcorn, The New
York Times, and Triffle's and Bloomie's catalogues.

The Provisional Government (meeting in you-know-
where) is drawing up a list of rationed items. Dental floss
was the first on the list, followed by press-on fingernails and
TV dinners. Gasoline is likely to follow. To meet our economic needs the Provisional Government (meeting you-
know-where) has recently issued the following economic
memorandum. Please stay tuned. This has been Norm

Runnion with a WFREE editorial, broadcasting from somewhere south of the West River.

FELLOW VERMONTERS: WHAT FOLLOWS IS A NARRA-
TIVE OF WHAT YOUR PROVISIONAL GOVERNMENT
(MEETING YOU-KNOW-WHERE) HAS APPROVED AS OUR
NEW ECONOMIC POLICY. FIRST OF ALL:

The Currency

The basic unit of Vermont's new money system will be the
ney, pronounced <u>neigh</u>. Historically, the word meant 'nay'
(and maybe it still should), and it is honored as our principal kind of money because it is the word most often heard
spoken at town meeting over the last two hundred years.
Only coincidentally, of course, is it <u>yen</u> spelled backward.

Five-ney, ten-ney, fourteen-ney, fifty-ney, and hundred-ney
bills will be issued. The fourteen-ney is being created to
confuse foreigners, allowing Vermonters an advantage in
the marketplace, and to remind us of the horrible mistake
we made when we let the Union join us in 1791.

Coins will be issued in four units, representing five percent of a ney, ten percent of a ney, one-quarter of a ney, and
one-half of a ney. Below are suggestions as to what they
might be called:

- The Ethan, the Ira, the Heman, and the Levi in honor of
  Vermont's four favorite brothers.
- The Holstein, the Jersey, the Ayrshire, and the Guernsey
  in honor of Vermont's four favorite cows.
- The North, the South, the East, and the West in honor of
  Vermont's four favorite directions.
- The Yup, the Nope, the Maybe, and the Won't in honor of
  Vermont's four favorite sentences.
- The Pile, the Run, the Cord, and the Fullcord in honor of
  Vermont's four favorite kinds of fuel.
- The Cough, the Sniffle, the Sneeze, and the Swallow in
  honor of Vermont's four favorite winter sports.

QUESTION 3
Well?

☐ YUP
☐ NOPE
☐ MAYBE
☐ NO IDEAR

We urge you to send us your favorite coin names before the presses roll on March 29. Remember, our address is: Provisional Government, Republic of Vermont (you-know-where).

Despite the vast, modern printing industry in Vermont, we do not intend simply to print money. We will back our money with real wealth — maple syrup, fancy grade.

As you know, more maple syrup is produced in Vermont than in any other state. Its value has increased remarkably as acid rain wipes out the maples of the Northeast. Maple syrup is intrinsically valuable and desirable. Like gold, it is very heavy and therefore hard to steal. Because it's liquid, it is even more difficult to rip off and, of course, has more liquidity.[3] Since it is sticky, it will be easy to trace if anyone does try to steal it. Finally, it is impossible to imitate. There is no "fool's maple syrup."

The Fort Knox of Vermont will be Graniteville.

There followed a short pause in the commentary, and the voice of Norm Runnion said, "Got that, Bentley Bentley?"

There the syrup will be pumped into worked-out quarries. Syrup wardens will take a squint at it, taste it for authentic-

[3]For this reason (and also because it is less susceptible to attacks by mice), it will not be boiled down into sugar cakes.

ity, and verify that it is fancy grade. Then it will be dumped, can by can, into the quarries.

Products

The flow of many raw materials has been reduced to a mere trickle since TUGWOS. It is therefore important that we begin to develop products that can be produced without outside support. Here are some ideas.

- Fresh Air. If the Japanese can sell canisters of air collected atop Mount Fuji, we can do the same almost anywhere, except near the Vicon Plant in Rutland or the Intervale in Burlington. Our fresh air could be pumped into "I Love Vermont" balloons and sold throughout the world.
- Granite Chips. From one ounce to five tons. They could be used as paperweights, necklaces, or doorstops, as volume fillers in fish tanks or toilets, or as anchors for boats. Certainly, they would be better than grainbags for extra weight in the trunk.
- Square inches of Vermont. If hucksters can sell stars in distant galaxies (with your own deed and coordinates) for a sawbuck, Vermonters ought to be able to get a lot more for the real thing. There are over six million square inches in an acre. There are hundreds, thousands, probably millions of people out there who want to have a "place in Vermont." As the Republic increasingly puts restrictions on condominiums, these square inches will become very popular. We can limit each customer to 100 square inches, enough land to make a hand print. Sub-division can be prohibited, and a 700 percent land gains tax can be levied on speculators.
- Dried sheep manure.
- High-priced ice cream.
- Trout. Vermont could specialize in troutburgers, perhaps export fast-fish franchises under the Leaping Rainbow label to Hong Kong, Tokyo, Bonn, Laos, and soon to Moscow.
- Bag Balm. Vermont should undertake a new marketing

campaign for this venerable Lyndonville product. Already widely used to soften cows' udders and chapped lips (on humans) and to treat heat rash, Bag Balm might earn a modest success by salving FUS's conscience for treating Vermont so badly.

- Butternuts. All over Vermont tons of these native nuts go to waste. Why? Because they're so damned hard to crack and there's so damned little there once you do. That's a lot like the Vermont economy. We could market these nuts because they're so tough. They could be sold as a health food — their benefit derived from the energy expended to break into them. "Vermont ... It's a Tough Nut to Crack" could become a selling line.

Agriculture

Free of federal influence, Vermont farmers will no longer be forced to cover the excesses of southern and western farmers. The dairy industry will flourish. Too long have we been duped into thinking that without federal price supports, Vermont's dairy industry would crumble. In the international market Vermonters will no longer subsidize air-conditioned barns in Georgia. Too, Vermont's status as an independent nation will enhance the attraction of its yogurt, cheese, milk, and ice cream.

At the same time Vermont should return to its roots. Sheep. Sheep do an even better job of clearing the land than do cattle. People of every stripe know that the single most important difference between Vermont and New Hampshire, aside from The Manchester Union-Leader, is the retention of open space in Vermont.

We suggest the creation of a national flock. This idea originated in the fertile mind of St. Johnsbury economist David Hale in the 1970s. An expanded version of the concept includes:

- National shepherds and shepherdesses to watch over the flock in the summer. High school and college students

could be given these healthy, back-to-the-earth jobs and
supplied with staffs, sheepdogs, tents, and supplies.
- Private landowners who wish to keep their lands open
could rent a part of the flock for a few weeks each summer
to graze their land.
- The government could use the flock in lieu of tractors to
cut the grass along public highways.
- Mutton could supply our hot lunch programs.

Tourism

As you know, tourism has been a staple of the Vermont
economy ever since Samuel de Champlain came in search
of the Loch Ness Monster and discovered Champ instead.
Ever since that time, visitors have reveled in Vermont's
"Special World" of physical beauty and individual liberty.

But we cannot dwell in the past. We are competing with
Disneyland, Six-Gun City, Six Flags over Texas, and the Pyra-
mid Mall in Plattsburgh. Why not develop a series of theme
parks focusing on Vermont's uniqueness? For instance:

- The first (thanks to David Hale, who thought up the idea)
could be Goddard College, a theme park from the era of
protest and the Beatles, called Sixties World. There tourists
could see original hippies in original tie-dye shirts, beads,
and moccasins, their hair uncut for decades. They could
buy posters of Danny the Red, Allen Ginsberg, and Janis
Joplin. They could attend a rap session, flash a peace
sign, and sigh 'Oh, wow!' twenty-five times in one hour.
In the summer they could watch braless softball on the
green. On Tuesday afternoons in July and August the park
could sponsor an authentic re-creation of a pot bust,
weather and availability of police permitting.
- Island Pond, now completely taken over by the Community Church, might be God's World.
- The Barre-Montpelier Road, replete with the gewgaws and
tacky baubles of American strip development, could be
roped off and advertised as Milton Friedman World, a
monument to untrammeled capitalism.

- In Royalton, we urge that great apologist for former President Reagan, Anthony Doria, to see if he can beat out Los Angeles for the rights to Ronnie's World.
- Vermont could well develop its own version of Parc Safari. After a moose fell in love with a Hereford cow in 1986, other unusual animal unions have been discovered. In Burke, a black bear and a Newfoundland found happy congress. In Thetford, a coyote and an Abyssinian cat howled duets for weeks on end. Why not round up all these weird combinations in one place and charge admission?

In talking to you about tourists, your Provisional Government hopes you will always remember that Vermonters have never fawned over them. In FUS, people are more concerned about their front yards than their backyards. Not Vermonters. We put cars, snowmobiles, firewood, tires, dogs, trucks, and farm machinery in the front yard. Why should we take anything around to the back of the house? Vermonters don't have anything to hide. Let's remember that, folks!

Postal Service

Whole nations have been supported by postage stamps: Monaco, Andorra, Fiji Islands, Cameroun, Sierra Leone, Lichtenstein, and others. Vermont should get in on this. The difference will be that thousands of causes and organizations will come to Vermont and be issued their own stamps, which they will purchase from the government. These organizations won't actually be here cluttering up the nation. All they will have to do is incorporate here, get themselves a mailing address, and pay taxes plus a fat fee for their stamps!

As a further incentive to those organizations, Vermont will offer them their own ZIP Codes. Again, a suitable fee will be charged for this service. Some groups may choose to locate not according to an individual ZIP but according to the name of a particular town or village. For example:

- Florence — the Italian-American Society
- Troy — Citizens for America (who always worry about betrayal from within)
- Wells — the Clean Water Coalition
- Readsboro — the National Library Association
- Morgan — the Morgan Horse Society, what else?
- Huntington — the NRA
- Hartland — the American Heart Association
- Grafton — the American Association of Retired Lobbyists
- Rockingham — the American Geological Society
- Duxbury — Ducks Unlimited
- Braintree — the Phi Beta Kappa Society or MENSA
- North Hero — the Oliver North Fan Club
- Bloomfield — the American Horticultural Society

There came a pause in the broadcast. Then Barre Jack was heard to say,

YOU HAVE BEEN LISTENING TO A SPECIAL REPORT FROM THE PROVISIONAL GOVERNMENT OF THE REPUBLIC OF VERMONT, (LOCATED YOU-KNOW-WHERE). WE NOW RETURN TO OUR REGULARLY SCHEDULED PROGRAMMING.

Deep under the White House in Washington, D.C., Robert McNearland leaned back in his chair with a sigh of relief. "That was a long one," he said.

"No! No! Don't relax!" cried Bentley Bentley. "It's coming. *This is it!*"

"What, sir?" said a young serviceman sitting at the controls of a computer.

"They're going to announce the location of their Provisional Government. It'll be in the title of the next record. I know it! All through that broadcast they kept saying the Provisional Government would meet 'you-know-where.' They were telling those hicks to stay tuned to be told where that place is. They'll reveal that right now. Give me that pencil. I've *got* to capture one of those meetings!" Bentley Bentley cocked an ear toward the radio.

Somewhere south of the West River, Norm Runnion hurriedly grabbed a stack of records and stepped into the control room of Radio Free Vermont. "Play these now," he said, and left.

Moments later he was in his car driving home. He liked this time of day. It stayed light longer in March, and he often saw deer on the edge of the woods. This evening he was in a particularly good mood. Turning on his radio, he settled back to listen to the songs he had given Jack to play: "Wichita Lineman," "Detroit City," "By the Time I Get to Phoenix," "Galveston," "Kansas City," and "North to Alaska."

"Take that," Norm Runnion said with a grin.

An hour later in Washington, D.C., Bentley Bentley collapsed on his cot, exhausted. "My God," he whispered, "they're meeting outside the country. Brilliant! But where? Which city is it? I'll have to hit them all. Book me on the first plane to Wichita!" he yelled to his staff as he bolted out the door to report this latest breakthrough to the President of the United States.

14

What to Do With Vermont Yankee?

April 2, 1991
(TUGWOS Plus 65)
The Windham County Courthouse: Morning Session

The meeting of the Provisional Government began at 9:15 with the question of what to do about Vermont Yankee. As if to break the immediate tension, one irate farmer jumped up in the rear and yelled, "Nuke 'em!" The titter of laughter was more nerves than mirth.

"Order!" snapped Madeline Harwood. "I think we agree that most Vermonters don't want the thing around anymore. For starters, the name Vermont Yankee is redundant." She smiled, and the audience laughed genuinely, even Angelo Linguini of Barre. "The question is, what to do with it?"

Proposals, arguments, and votes began to come from the floor almost immediately. They were duly recorded by Jim Douglas, who had been elected Republic Clerk the day before—thereby (as only he and a few others knew) becoming the most powerful person in Vermont.

- We could make plutonium for our own nuclear arsenal. Better yet, we could *threaten* to make plutonium and then agree not to—for a price. (Yup 16, nope 246.)
- We could turn it into a fish hatchery. It's situated perfectly on the Connecticut River and would be an excel-

lent place to breed bullheads and suckers. (Yup 142, nope 163; Trout Unlimited had lobbied successfully.)

- We could sponsor an essay contest between former State Senator Peter Welch and Interim Ambassador to the UN Ralph Wrong on the subject "How to Tell Vermont from Massachusetts" and give it to the loser.[1] (Yup 78, nope 129.)
- We could turn it into a southern campus for the University of Vermont, the second-largest producer of nuclear waste in the state. (Yup 1, nope 234; the southern Vermont lobby didn't seem to want UVM down there.)
- We could turn it into a new movie-making facility to service the increasingly numerous motion-picture producers who are using northern New England to make movies. We could rename it "Hollyglow." (Yup 14, nope 240.)

After five votes and no resolution, Archibald Twiddlewart, a man who had attended sixty-two straight town meetings in Brookline, Vermont, arose and cleared his throat. People immediately reached for their NODOZ.

"Why not *cause* a meltdown?" he began. "When the China Syndrome occurs, all of New England could use the resulting hole through the center of the earth to China as a giant landfill dump. Situated as it is on the very southeast corner of the state, it's as accessible to Boston and Hartford as it is to Burlington. The new Republic of Vermont could then finally fulfill a dream that has lurked in the unconscious of every citizen since the early days of the environmental movement.

"Is there a Vermonter alive who has never placed six putrid plastic bags into the trunk or onto the backseat of his car, traveled to the dump on a Saturday morning, and flung those black bombs into a sea of domestic barf? Then paid an attendant an exorbitant tribute while dodging sea-

---

[1] The winner would receive a one-way ticket to Lowell, Massachusetts.

gull dung[2] from a mass swirling in the heavens above that would have made Alfred Hitchcock shudder?"

It was Archibald's best speech. His neighbors from Brookline cheered him on. "Atta boy, Archie!" they yelled.

"What Vermonter driving home from such a place — windows open even at twenty degrees below zero — has not fantasized a huge infinite hole in the ground into which might be tossed all the world's garbage bags with them-selves collecting a modest toll for each bag — a hole thou-sands of miles deep with a fiery hell at the center and with the assurance that if anything did get through the earth's core, it would only end up in China?"

Archie sat down to thunderous applause. His wife smiled approvingly. With the meeting thus relaxed, serious discus-sion resumed. Thirty minutes later, the assembly approved (289–3) the following:

> Be it resolved that the buildings and grounds of Vermont Yankee be immediately converted into a great, year-round flea market (still and more appropriately bearing the name Vermont Yankee) in which to sell federal equipment confis-cated during TUGWOS — from postal vehicles to paper shred-ders to red tape.

"But what will we do with the nuclear waste?" someone yelled from the rear.

In an instant, Archie was on his feet. "Put it on barges and float it down the Connecticut. *They* put it here — let them figure it out!" He didn't wait for Mrs. Harwood. "All those in favor?" he cried, raising his fist toward the ceiling.

"Yup!" roared every soul in the Windham County Court-house.

"Dinner's served," said Madeline.

[2] Often it's crow dung.

15

One Out, One In

Population Policy
April 2, 1991
The Windham County Courthouse: Afternoon Session

It used to be that Vermont's harsh climate and poverty were enough to limit the state's population. In the 1950s, when the interstate highways were first planned, officials believed that they would lower the population further since many natives would use them to escape. But then people began to use the highways to get *in*! The rest is history.

Soon after TUGWOS, it was apparent that Vermont was even more desirable than before. Something had to be done. Within weeks the Provisional Government had announced a six-week "get-out-while-you-can" period. Anyone left in Vermont after that time was declared a full citizen of the Republic and issued a new birth certificate, entitled "Born Green." It also asked its citizens for suggestions on whether and how the nation should limit its population.

When the pie and coffee were finished and the PG meeting was called back into session at 1:35 on April 2, the first order of business was population policy. John Carnahan was moderator.

He began, "Anyone been down at the south end of I-91 lately near the 'Unwelcome to Vermont' sign?"

"Ah, yes!" said the audience knowingly.

"Then you've seen and heard what I have. Thousands of people encamped on the Massachusetts side, yelling, screaming, clamoring to get in. I think we agree"—he, like Madeline, knew how to keep a meeting on schedule—"that we've got to have a population policy."

"Never!" yelled Frank Bryan from the back of the room. "Tyranny!"

Carnahan ignored him, as did everyone else at the meeting. "I thought we'd begin by solving our internal population question and then move on to immigration policy. Everyone agreed? Fine," he said without missing a beat. "First of all, let me read you a short list of some of the proposals we've received from our request for suggestions:

- I think parents should be licensed. Anyone who wants children should have to prove they know how to be parents, much as you have to show you can drive a car before you are allowed on the highways. To have children, you must also demonstrate you can care for them, just as you must show you can make the payments before you can get a mortgage to buy a house.

- Keep your noses out of the population business. Any government that's powerful enough to license parents and mortgage kids is too damned powerful.
- The nation's population should never be allowed to exceed 600,000. Period.
- If it's a choice between condoms and condominiums, it's no contest.
- Keep the government out of living rooms and bedrooms. Jeez! We didn't create a People's Republic of Vermont.
- License parents and mortgage kids as long as it's guaranteed I will be named to the license and mortgage boards.
- Let's go back to freezing the old folks.
- The third child born to any family must be put in a basket and floated down the Connecticut River in March.
- Hell. We're Yankees, ain't we? Let's go into the kid business. Vermonters should be able to have as many kids as they want. But they can only *keep* two. Since FUS doesn't have enough kids down there, we'll provide an international baby market. The money would help fill the nation's treasury. Diplomatic relations with FUS would be improved, since they don't seem to know whether children are property or not and it's raising hell in their legal system.
- Blow the hind end off the next flatlander that comes up here, that's what we should do.
- Not a damned thing. It's none of my business, and none of yours, either.
- Make it a law that any man that doesn't do night feedings and diapers can be jailed for twenty years without parole.

The discussion of these and other suggestions throughout the afternoon was hot and heavy. Finally, at 4:15 it was agreed that Vermont's population be allowed to rise to 750,000. After that, it was zero population growth. One out, one in. Vermont families could have as many kids as they wanted as long as it wasn't more than two. Except for the following:

- Any family can have three children as long as one of them grows up to become a farmer.
- Anyone with a bumper sticker that reads "Have you hugged your kid today?" may not have any.

- Farmers can have one kid for every twenty milkin' cows.
- No family with more than two kids, and no single parent with more than one, may count any extras for tax purposes. The government will not subsidize large families. On the other hand, in case of war, no family may have more than two children drafted into the armed forces. People who have had *no* children (even though they could have) will be drafted themselves. The government will not risk the children of citizens to defend DINKs (Double Income *No Kids*). If Vermont needs defending with blood, you got two choices — send your kids, or go yourself.

"Now," said Carnahan, "I know it's late, but let's see if we can resolve the immigration problem before we adjourn."

"Sure," snorted Ben Smith from Addison. "That's how you guys always do it. Save the good stuff till last when us farmers have to go milk."

"Do I hear a motion we adjourn until nine-thirty tomorrow morning?" asked Carnahan, clearly embarrassed.

"Wait." It was Sam Hand, all the way from Burlington. "I bring word from Bill Mares. His sources report that that despicable, dastardly dog of disruption, Colonel Bentley Bentley, has flown back to Washington from Nome. Seems he'd gone 'North to Alaska' " — Hand paused while the audience giggled — "and he now knows we aren't up there!" More laughter, harder this time. "That means," continued Hand, now stern, "that we are again in peril and we must again move our meeting place." (Groans.) "But, after all, that's only proper. In the early days of the original Vermont Republic" — cheers — "the capital was moved periodically. We should do the same, for our own safety if nothing else." (Murmurs of approval.)

"But where, Sam?"

"In deference to the mountain rule,[1]" said Hand, "the next meeting should be on the western side of the mountains." (Nods of agreement.) "How about Burlington?" (Hoots of disapproval.) Hand continued good-naturedly. "Okay, how about the First Congregational Church in Middlebury?"

"Good," said Eric Davis, a professor from Middlebury College.

"But what about the separation of church and state?" called out someone.

"Ah, to hell with it," came the answer from a very neat older lady in the first row. She stood and faced the meeting. "He said the First Congregational Church! This is Vermont, and that's our church!"

"Right on!" yelled Father Patrick Delaney.

"Done," said Carnahan. "Adjourned until tomorrow morning at nine-thirty in Middlebury, when the first item on the Warning will be immigration policy."

"Hey!" yelled Frank Bryan. "We gotta *vote* on that." But no one paid attention to him in their rush for the door.

[1] The tradition of electing governors from one side of the state to the other in perfect rotation. It began in 1870 and ended in 1944.

16

Who Goes There?

Immigration Policy
April 3, 1991
(TUGWOS Plus 66)
Washington, D.C.

Lieutenant Colonel Bentley Bentley hovered over his radio in the basement of the White House. "Where's Haig?" he yelled.

"He's hitting the heavy bag again."

"Good. The less he knows, the better."

"True," said Rear Admiral Poinsettia, a recent appointment to Bentley Bentley's staff.

"Listen up," said Bentley Bentley.

GOOD MORNING, VERMONT. THIS IS NORM RUNNION FROM SOMEWHERE SOUTH OF THE WEST RIVER. THIS MORNING WE ARE BRINGING YOU LIVE COVERAGE OF THE PROVISIONAL GOVERNMENT'S IMPORTANT DELIBERATIONS ON IMMIGRATION POLICY FROM YOU-KNOW-WHERE.

Hello. I'm Mal Boright speaking to you directly from you-know-where. There are still a few pews (damn) seats left, so if you're in the area, why don't you come on over? The Moderator for the Day is Howard Pumper, who operates

Jessie's Truck Stop, south of town. Father Patrick Delaney
will say the opening prayer.

"In the name of the Father, the Son, and the Holy Spirit.
Father in Heaven, bring your blessing on this Republic and
the people gathered here today. Bring them wisdom. For as
the Israelites sought the promised land of Canaan, they
too seek ..."

In Washington, D.C., Bentley Bentley, still suffering
from jet lag, leaped into the air and grabbed Poinsettia by
the lapels. "That's it!" he yelled. "*That's it! They're in
Canaan, Vermont, at the Catholic Church! It's gotta be!*
That rabble-rousing son-of-a-bitch Frank Bryan claims he
was born there. It's next door to New Hampshire! I want
fifty choppers. We'll hit those hicks at two this afternoon
and have their whole blasted government down here by
suppertime. *Hot damn!*"

Poinsettia asked, "Shall we tell Haig?"

Bentley Bentley didn't open his mouth. But his eyes said,
Don't be stupid!

Meanwhile, back at the First Congregational Church in
Middlebury, Don Dufus of Grand Isle was finishing a
prepared statement. "The Republic is firmly in place, and
only yesterday we agreed on a population policy. But even
as I speak, thousands of immigrants are swarming toward
our borders. The Rio Grande will seem like the Berlin Wall
compared to Lake Champlain, the Connecticut, and Lake
Memphremagog; and these waters *ice over.* Why be a wet-
back when you can walk across on snowshoes?

"First of all, we need an Ellis Island. I suggest
Horseneck Island in Lake Memphremagog. The wall of the
induction center could bear the inscription:

> Give me your homesick,
> Your befuddled — those longing to be free,
> Send these, the over-governed, 'sick and tired'
> to me!

"Next, we'll need some criteria for admission, in order of importance. Top priority will go to any *direct* blood relatives of Vermont families who were trapped outside the state during TUGWOS. Top priority also goes to the citizens of Paramus, New Jersey (they've suffered enough); to anyone with the last name Wheeler; and to anyone from Switzerland—if they bring their bank accounts. Finally, Vermonters retired and living in Florida get top priority. We understand why you left. It *is* cold up here in the winter. But this is your home. If you want to come back, you're always welcome.

"Second priority goes to any Texan who is willing to say the following: 'I (name) concede that Vermonters have more guts than Texans, and it is also true that if it were flattened out, Vermont would be bigger than Texas.' Also to anyone from Brooklyn who will promise not to run for Mayor of Burlington; to any member of the 1987 Boston Celtics; and to anyone who guarantees they will wait ten years before they start telling us how to redesign Vermont to the specifications of the places they left behind.

"Finally, the outright rejects. For instance:

- Any citizen of West Virginia. (Hey, you got a damned good place to live where you are. You don't need us.)[1]
- Alan Alda and Sam Donaldson. (One believes in wimp power; the other believes in blowhard power.)
- Ronald and Nancy Reagan. (You had a chance to make it right with us in the 1980s, but you let those corporate Republicans take over. Sorry.)

"Obviously, we'll have to let in students to study at the University of Vermont or it will collapse financially and President Lattie Coor will have to work for a living. Plus, we'll need people to come in and work and share their expertise with us. Most of all, we'll have to let people visit for humanitarian reasons. People can come from Los Angeles to clean out their lungs, from New York City to

[1] And by the way, keep those good tunes coming up from WWVA in Wheeling.

clean out their minds, from Kuwait to clean out their
pockets.

"Finally, I have in my possession David Hale's remark-
able document, 'The Republic of Vermont: A Modest Proposal.' Hale's ingenious suggestion will in one fell swoop
regulate immigration, protect the environment, enhance
citizenship, and bring untold wealth to the new nation.
With his permission, I would like to read it to you now.

The Republic of Vermont could issue every present citizen
and all newly born Vermonters a passport which guaranteed
their right to live here. If an outsider wanted to move to Vermont, they would have to purchase one of these passports for
whatever price the market would fetch.

Such a system of immigration control would have three
major advantages; the first environmental, the second economic, and the third social.

The environmental advantage is that we would be able to
keep population growth in some reasonable state of balance,
as the number of people coming approximately equaled the
number of people going. If there were labor shortages, we
could always cheat a little by issuing special passports for
people with skills greatly in demand. If there was a glut in certain professions, as there is now with lawyers, we could also
restrict entry somewhat. But 99% of the time, the marketplace would decide who could live here.

The economic advantage would be the opportunity, at last
provided, to put a price tag on the Vermont way of life. One
of the great problems in protecting the Vermont environment
today is our inability to put a cash value on it. As developers
destroy our hillsides and valleys, every Vermonter knows in
his heart that something precious has been lost. But the average person is confused when he protests because economists
and real estate men tell him that such destruction is making
society richer.

The hitch, of course, is that our present system of measur-
ing economic advancement consists of a one-entry, one-sided
balance sheet. We record increases in the quantity of goods
and services produced but make no offsetting entry for their
potential destructive effect on the quality of life. We could, in

theory, appear to be growing richer as our community is converted into a junkyard.

The Vermont passport market offers one way out of this dilemma. It could put a price tag on our countryside and way of life. If our passports sold for ten thousand dollars apiece, with five hundred thousand cards available, we would know that the value of our environment was about five billion dollars. Each new bid in the marketplace would tell us whether the Vermont quality of life was improving or deteriorating. A decline in passport prices would lead to a storm of newspaper criticism about how Vermont was being destroyed by ruinous development. An increase in bids would produce praise from all for the sensible way in which Vermont was conducting its affairs, especially in balancing economic and environmental concerns.

It is possible that a few liberal individuals will object to such a system on grounds of conscience (citizenship should not be sold) but they could find consolation by taking ten thousand dollars for their passports and moving to a place where citizenship is free.

The last advantage of the passport market is social and in some respects political. It will remind people that citizenship carries responsibilities as well as privileges. The daily publication of Vermont passport prices in the newspaper will give everyone the highest incentive possible to be a good citizen because any socially destructive action would generate bad publicity about Vermont and reduce the desire for outsiders to buy our passports. This could result in some vigilantism in the short run as private citizens make extra efforts to guard their passport values, but in the long run it would increase everyone's personal freedom considerably.

When Dufus had finished, he turned to the moderator. "Mr. Moderator, I would now like to place this and the rest of my plan before the meeting as a motion."

"Do I hear a second?" asked the moderator.

"So moved."

"Discussion?" (Silence.)

"Hearing none: All those in favor, say yup."

"Yup!" yelled the crowd.

"All those opposed?"

"Nope!" yelled Myron Blacktopper, president of the Vermont Association of Real Estate Dealers.

"The yups have it. May I have a motion to adjourn?"

"So moved."

"All those in favor!"

"Yup!"

"Against?" (Silence.)

Sometimes a lot happens in a Vermont town meeting very, very quickly, indeed.

Outside the First Congregational Church, Bill Mares took Father Patrick Delaney aside. "Did you mention Canaan, Father?"

"Yup."

"Good," said Mares.

A Secessionist Jedi
George Aiken

In 1938 George Aiken wrote an incandescent volume
entitled *Speaking from Vermont,* which will live forever as
an early and courageous foreshadowing of TUGWOS.

> The most distinguishing feature of life in Vermont just now
> is the determination of our people to do things for themselves
> and to learn how those things can be done better and more
> economically.
>
> The first ideal that prompted the settlement of Vermont
> was the love of liberty. It was this ideal which prompted the
> founders of our state to forswear allegiance to any government
> or any other state or colony. It was that ideal which prompted
> the settlers of 1777 to set up their own form of government; to
> write their own Constitution without the aid of a lawyer . . .
> and it is this love of liberty that today prompts Vermont to
> revolt against the approach toward that type of centralized
> government which history has so often proved undesirable.
>
> These principles of loving liberty, of self-reliance, of thrift
> and of liberalism have inspired Vermonters to the greatest,
> most satisfying of all ideals — self-respect. We are not
> ashamed. We do not think it old-fashioned or reactionary to
> insist upon the principles of local self-government. We believe
> that remote control of government is antiquated and not
> progressive.

Aiken fought to protect Vermont's natural resources
from both private power companies and the federal government.[1] He spoke as follows against a congressional act that
would have prohibited interstate compacts for flood control along the Connecticut River and turned ownership of
"all Vermont's natural resources" to the federal government.
"No further evidence is necessary to show the determination

[1] Proving his genius for understanding that in politics as in farming
and, indeed, in life itself, the question of appropriate scale is key.

[of the federal government] to abolish state lines and state existence as political units," he said and continued:

Vermont is a small state. Only a few are smaller; yet up among our green hills for a hundred and sixty years there has existed a love of liberty and a spirit of self-reliance second to none in the world. For fourteen years we existed as an independent commonwealth, owing allegiance to no other government.

Never wealthy, except in those things that money cannot buy, we have practised from the very beginning a policy of paying our debts and doing without those things we could not honestly afford. We are successfully practising this policy today because we still control our natural resources.

And now it is proposed by those high in authority to take from Vermont, without her consent, the means and the rights by which her people have supported themselves for over a century and a half.

What Vermont asks, and I appeal for the assistance of the other forty-seven [sic] states in this matter, is the right to handle purely local affairs in our own way; to enter into agreements with any of our sister states on such matters as may concern us alone; to continue, without interference, adhering to the principles of industry, self-reliance, self-respect; and to remain solvent.

Do they believe that the ideals of thrift and independence up in New England have been forgotten overnight? Or that a desire to cast aside the responsibility and authority of local self-government has been created by a few years of tremendously increasing national debt, which we feel that sometime must and should be paid?

We didn't let them get away with it, thanks mostly to George Aiken.

17

Chaos in Canaan

April 3, 1991
Canaan, Vermont   1:30 P.M.

Frank Bryan slammed his 1964 flatbed GMC pickup to a halt on the bridge over the Connecticut River between West Stewartstown, New Hampshire, and Canaan, Vermont. He grabbed a sign that read WELCOME TO ISLAND POND from the back and quickly hammered it over the "Welcome to Canaan, Vermont" sign. Jumping back into the cab, he hooked the shockcord that held the driver's door shut and gunned the old truck toward the home of Bea Holmes, who at age ninety-three was still Canaan's most distinguished citizen.

Beside him on the seat was a copy of *The Newport Daily Express,* which, like every other newspaper in the Republic that day, carried the PG's list of possibilities for the Republic's new motto. Bryan had always liked New Hampshire's awfully well — "Live Free or Die." He mused that people in states like Massachusetts ridiculed it. Hell, Massachusetts's motto was "By the Sword We Seek Peace. But Peace Only Under Liberty." Give that to Mares, thought Bryan, and he'd edit it down to what it really means — live free or die.

The finalists from the high-school motto contest that the PG had sponsored and that Vermonters would vote on were:

- "Freedom and Unity"
- "Drink Milk or Die"
- "Damn the Torpedoes, Full Speed Ahead"
- "Independence Is Better Than Riches"[1]
- "You Can't Get Here From There"
- "Whoa!"
- "We Waste Litterers"
- "To Be Rather Than To Seem"[2]
- "We Brake for Nothin' "
- "It Grows as it Goes"[3]
- "Save the Bales"
- "Woodchuck Power"
- "Mountaineers Are Always Free"[4]
- "Liberty, Liberty, Liberty, Liberty, Liberty . . ."

Bryan hurriedly drove down the main street of Canaan, past the "Island Pond General Store," the "Island Pond Town Library," and the "Island Pond Town Clerk's Office." There was even a little restaurant whose name had been changed to "The Buck & Doe." Several members of the Hill Farmer Brigade who had helped waved as he went

[1] This item was placed on the list directly from *Talk Less and Say More* by Wolfgang Mieder.

[2] The motto of North Carolina.

[3] New Mexico's motto.

[4] It's West Virginia's now, but we could take it.

by. Thinking about this little Northeast Kingdom town, the place if not of his birth, at least of his conception, Bryan made up his mind on the motto issue before he pulled into Bea Holmes's yard. He'd vote for the old one, "Freedom and Unity."

Bea was ready. She climbed into the cab, and Bryan slammed her door—three times.

"You know what you're doing?" he asked her as they headed for the Catholic church.

"Sure I do. There'll be a bunch of soldiers or other kinds of strangers run into the church. They'll wonder where everyone is. They may ask for Father Delaney. I'm to say there isn't any meeting today in Island Pond, and no Father Delaney, either."

"And they'll be surprised you said Island Pond." Bryan waited.

"I know. I know," said Bea, irritated. "I'm to act like they're lost flatlanders and tell them they're twenty miles southwest of Canaan in Island Pond and that the Connecticut River, over there, is the Clyde. Then I'm to walk out of the church with them, point southeast into New Hampshire in the general direction of Dixville Notch, and say, 'Canaan, Vermont's over there!' "

"Great!" exclaimed Bryan. "Look, Bea, if they ask you why the Clyde River's east of town instead of west, tell them it *surrounds* Island Pond. Say something like, 'That's why they call it *Island* Pond, dummy!' "

Bea smiled.

"The real question is whether or not they'll believe the Mohawk River over at Dixville Notch is the Connecticut. Good thing these are FUS officials. They'll be lost. And their maps'll be fifty years old!"

"One more thing," he said as he opened the door of his truck for Bea—with her pushing from the inside—at Our Lady of Avignon Catholic Church. "There'll be a group of people coming in with kerchiefs and beards, and they'll have a sign that says 'Repent Now' or something. They'll probably start praying and ask the FUS people to pray with them to save their souls. We've told them to leave you alone and to concentrate on the FUS. But be prepared."

"My soul's my own business," snapped Bea, and she disappeared inside the church.

An hour and fifteen minutes later, Bryan was laughing so hard, he had to hold his knees together in the phone booth.

"Mares?"

"Yeah. Control yourself, Bryan!"

"You're a genius, Bill! They roared in here out of the sky like a swarm of June mosquitoes. Fifty of them! You couldn't hear yourself think! Bentley Bentley lands on the lawn of the church—"

"Where'd the other copters go?"

"Three landed, the others just circled the town. Bea was beautiful! Bentley comes out of the church all confused and looks across the street at the 'Island Pond Post Office.' Then he's hit with these seven Jesus freaks. You can see the wheels turning in his little head.

"Suddenly he yells to his radio man, 'She's right. I heard about this town in an intelligence briefing. Radio the others, tell them to head twenty miles *east* across the Clyde over there. Take me up, boys.' And away they go, trailing off over the White Mountains toward Dixville Notch."

"What happened over there?"

"It was beautiful. Kunin had found the place, all right. There isn't much of it, but she'd put some signs up, and she staged a town meeting in an old barn she converted to a Catholic church."

"How?"

"Told them she was making a movie about Vermont but there wasn't any Vermont left in Vermont so she had to come to New Hampshire. She got extras from all the surrounding towns, spent yesterday training them, and had 'em packed in there like sardines, 210 of them."

"And—Bryan, for god's sake, stop laughing!"

"Bill, they're all on their way to Washington! I can't *stand* it. Kunin pulled it off! She even told them the raid was part of the movie and that they should resist a little but then get into the copters."

"FUS captured its own town and took it back to Washington," said Mares, his grin clearly visible over the telephone wire. "They'll be ripped!"

"Then tell 'em to TUGWOS," said Bryan, and hung up.

Rather Dan began a live interview with Rear Admiral John Poinsettia at 7:15 P.M. on April 3 on *The CBS Evening News.* "It is our understanding that forces of the United States attacked Dixville Notch, New Hampshire, at three-ten this afternoon."

"Yes, they did, Rather."

"Why?"

"It was a mistake. We intended to hit Canaan, Vermont, but our troops got lost in the fog."

"Is that the truth? We heard those Vermonters snookered you again."

"As far as I can recollect, it's the truth. Remember, it happened over three hours ago."

"Governor Sununu is understandably very upset. The word we have is that New Hampshire may secede, too. What's your comment?"

"Nasty rumors, Rather. As of this moment, New Hampshire's with us a thousand percent."

"We've had no word from the Oval Office. When will President Haig speak to the nation on this?"

"Well, Rather, he hasn't been told yet, and the decision whether to tell him ever has not been made. It will depend on how New Hampshire behaves. If everything turns out all right, we'll probably not bother him with it. But if they do leave the Union, we'll have to reconsider that judgment, of course."

Rather, for once, was speechless. "But—but surely he watches newscasts like this!" he stammered.

"No, Rather, he doesn't. The President doesn't like you guys."

18

"Gov'ment"

April 17, 1991
(TUGWOS Plus 80)
Montpelier, Vermont

Washington, D.C. went batshit. Congress was like an anthill busted open by a bear. Committees launched a dozen or more investigations and public hearings into Canaangate, dwarfing those of Watergate and Iranamuck. Crisis raged in the White House.

The Republic took this opportunity to hold a constitutional convention in Montpelier to debate and decide Vermont's ultimate form of government. The proceedings were carried live on Radio Free Vermont.

By April 17, 1991, the following document had been forged on the people's anvil. Later that summer it would be submitted to the voters for their yup or nope. Meanwhile, the Provisional Government continued its work.

THE CONSTITUTION OF THE REPUBLIC OF VERMONT

Preamble

Once upon a time in old Vermont, a city boy was brought up by some Fresh Air–type of fund for a few weeks' vacation to Vermont. For the first time in his life, he discovered a toad. He was fascinated by the little critter and kept poking it with a stick to get it to hop, until finally a local lad, who thought the toad was tired of such treatment, said, "Leave that tud alone."

"Why should I?" the city kid asked. "It's my toad, ain't it?"

"No," said the other youngster, "in Vermont he's his own tud!"[1]

Principles of Governance

- "War is too important to be left up to the generals."[2]
- "Those that labor in the earth are the chosen people of God." (Thomas Jefferson)
- "Private property ought to be subservient to the public uses when necessity requires it." (from the Constitution of the old State of Vermont)[3]
- " 'Tis our true policy to steer clear of permanent

[1] From *What the Old-Timer Said* by Allen R. Foley, a spiritual ancestor of the Vermont Independence Movement.

[2] The Vermont Corollary: Education is too important to be left up to the educators; the environment too important to be left up to the environmentalists; highways too important to be left up to highway engineers and construction companies. Most important, democracy is too important to be left up to the politicians.

[3] Be it further resolved that when we say *necessity* we mean NECESSITY, goddamnit!

alliances, with any portion of the foreign world."
(George Washington)

- "The gods of the hills are not the gods of the valleys."
  (Ethan Allen)
- "The government . . . is a device for maintaining in
  perpetuity the rights of the people, with the ultimate
  extinction of all privileged classes." (Calvin Coolidge)
- "No man should be allowed to own any land that he does
  not use." (Robert Ingersoll)
- "Politics and the pulpit are terms that have little agree-
  ment." (Edmund Burke)
- "In every generation there has to be some fool who will
  speak the truth as he sees it." (Boris Pasternak)
- "Better we lose the election than mislead the people."
  (Adlai Stevenson)
- "There will never be a generation of great men until there
  has been a generation of free women — of free mothers."
  (Robert Ingersoll)
- "Vermont is not for sale." (Thomas Salmon)
- "The best way to kill something in Vermont is to mandate
  it." (Richard Snelling)
- "Hain't we got all the fools in town on our side? And
  hain't that a big enough majority in any town?" (Huckle-
  berry Finn)

Punishment

The punishment for all crimes in Vermont shall be the
same — the liqua-store treatment. The condemned will sit
over a dunking pool, defined as a liqua-store manure pit
filled to the brim with the real thing. Volunteers will then
throw baseballs at a triggering device. The severity of the
crime will determine the following:

- Where the pit will be located (the village green, the
  Barton Fair, and so on).
- How many baseballs each volunteer gets.
- How close they can be when they throw.
- Whether or not snorkels, flippers, or wetsuits may be
  used.

- The kind of cows producing the manure.
- Whether the condemned must be fully clothed.

The Bill of Wrongs

- It shall be unlawful in Vermont to employ a gardener.
- "A person can not be compelled to give evidence against himself" (from the Constitution of the old State of Vermont) unless the following conditions apply:
  a. he is caught in the act
  b. he is suspected of stealing maple syrup
  c. any damned fool knows he did it
- Discrimination because of sexual preference, habits, or proclivities practiced in private is strictly forbidden. Anyone caught doing so shall be forced to roll an egg between Greensboro and Lyndonville during mud season.
- No law shall be made respecting the establishment of religion, except for the adoption of the Congregational Church as the official national church. That's okay.
- The freedom to buy a public office with money your grandparents left you may be protected under the Constitution of FUS, but Vermonters know that this has nothing to do with freedom and plenty to do with injustice. Therefore, any candidate caught spending more than the cost of a pint of milk per voter in his or her campaign will get the liqua-store treatment.[4]
- It is unconstitutional in Vermont to discharge a firearm from inside the house. However, guns may be shot from barns, cars, horseback, or any other damned place.
- The government cannot interfere in a citizen's right to free speech. Freedom of speech is absolute. Almost.

[4] For instance, under the old Vermont system the following would have applied in 1986:

Office	Number of Voters	Cost of a Pint of Milk	Total Expenditure Allowed
Governor	196,716	.35	$68,850.60
State Senator from Chittenden County	14,016	.35	4,905.60
School Director Town of Charleston	117	.35	40.95

a. You can't cry "Fire!" in a closed theater or "Wood-chucks are vermin!" at the Tunbridge Fair.[5]
b. No one under eighteen can give advice to anyone, anytime, anywhere, about anything.
c. Children may not be exploited to promote products on television or candidates for public office.
d. It shall be unlawful to use the following words or phrases in public:

- "by my authority"
- "compromise"
- "the bottom line"
- "if it ain't broke, don't fix it"
- *anything* "gate"
- "surrender"
- "parental bonding"
- "schmooze"
- "comfort zone"
- "have a nice day"
- "level playing field"
- "quality time"
- "plausible deniability"

The Executive Branch

The Chief Executive Officer of Vermont shall be called the Moderator of the Republic and shall serve a term of one year, with a limit of one term per decade. The election of the Moderator shall take place during the airing of Vermont ETV's annual auction. Candidates will auction off goods, and the one who sells the most will be declared the winner.

The Moderator's mansion shall be located in the trailer park nearest the Moderator's home. The Moderator must live there as a reminder that the living is still tough for many working people.

No one living outside Vermont in 1987 shall be elected Moderator until the election of 2010.

[5] Actually you *can* but don't expect help from the constables at Tunbridge.

Powers denied the Moderator:

- Turning over the government to someone else while they continue to campaign for things they didn't dare mention during the election.
- Calling a special session of the legislature.
- Revealing a new program immediately *after* an election and then traveling the country campaigning for it.
- Saying "I've appointed a committee to study the problem. It will report after the election."
- Sending police to raid the homes of citizens simply because they belong to a particular church.
- Running for another office while still Moderator.

Powers given the Moderator:

- Waving the checkered flag at Thunder Road's "Milk Bowl."
- Picking up the first dead skunk on Green Up Day.
- Declaring a state of emergency—but only if there is one. No state of emergency shall ever be declared on the first day of deer season, for any snow-related problems whatsoever, or during the month of July.
- Delivering a State of the Nation address once a year to the legislature. Any Moderator who speaks more than ten minutes will be ignored.
- Resigning whenever they feel like it.

Impeachment

The Moderator may be impeached for any reason whatsoever.

Oath of Office

"I'll do what I can."

The Bill of Rights

Vermonters have the right to do anything they damned well please as long as they don't bother anybody. As some philosopher once said, "Your right to hit me ends where my nose begins."

Others distinguish between the right to harvest one's own garden and a neighbor's freedom to let his hogs harvest that garden early; between the right to walk a country road in peace and the freedom of a power-crazed eight-year-old to charge down that road on a 75-horsepower ATV with no muffler; between the right to eat at a restaurant in breathable air and another diner's freedom to blow cigarette smoke in your salad.

If we'd only be sensible, we'd need no Bill of Rights. The following should therefore be considered illustrations only:

- Vermont farmers may spread manure anytime, anyplace, in any manner they see fit, as long as they spread it on their own land. Liquid manure is outlawed. The odor kills sparrows in midflight. If a spreader slings manure over fifty feet out the back, it is unlawful for it to turn within fifty feet of a public highway. Unless you need to. Then—well, what the hell.
- All Vermonters have the right to be late to work if it is mud season, twenty-five degrees below zero or worse, the first day of deer or trout season, the Monday following the Tunbridge Fair, or the last day of deer season.
- Any Vermonter who can hear a portable radio or tape

HI, BOSS? I'LL
BE LATE..
RIGHT.
MUD.

recorder that is being played across a highway or street at least two lanes wide may cross the street, seize it, and smash it to smithereens on the ground.

- Any Vermonter who is kept waiting in a doctor's office more than a half-hour has the right to full compensation for their time at an hourly rate that shall equal the average hourly wage of Vermont doctors.
- Vermonters have the right to give wrong directions to foreigners traveling in Vermont.
- Vermont citizens have the right to drive down the middle of any unpaved road as slowly as they please. Anyone caught honking at a Vermonter doing this will be subject to an on-the-spot citizen's arrest.
- Vermonters have the right to honk at fancy riding horses and riders if, in the mind of the Vermonter, they give you the "me and my horse are more important than you and your truck" look.[6]
- Vermonters have a right to rev up their chain saws any time they please. But only nerds would do this before 5 A.M. in a residential neighborhood.
- Any Vermonter who mistakenly fells a tree across a public highway will be given plenty of time to clean it up.
- Vermonters have the inalienable right to build anything on their own property they want to and to keep anything they want to in whatever they build—hens, hogs, cattle, whatever. There is no such thing as visual pollution in Vermont—any damn fool knows that. Also, if the neighbors don't like the smell, too bad. This right, however, carries the following duties:
  a. If one of your critters wanders away and lands in somebody's freezer, have the good sense to keep your mouth shut.
  b. If the smell gets too bad, you must clean up or get rid of your stock. You will know when it gets too bad

[6] Anyone in a car who does not give wide berth to a kid on a nag will be given the liqua-store treatment at the Tunbridge Fair.

because your neighbors will gang up on you and beat you to a pulp—and you'll deserve it.

c. No Vermonter may keep any living thing that doesn't have feet, wings, or fins.

The Legislative Branch

The chief legislative body will be the Town Meeting of the Republic, which will continue to meet when and where it wants and do pretty much what it wants—providing the towns themselves, which are the real seat of power, approve. Anything left over will be decided by a new national legislature. Vermont shall return to its tradition of giving each town and city equal strength in the House of Representatives. Arlington is no less important than Montpelier; Athens is equal to Burlington. Readsboro is as significant as Rutland, Monkton as Middlebury, Barton as Brattleboro, Hartland as Hartford.

The Vermont legislature shall consist of one chamber, with three representatives from each city and town. Its presiding officer shall be called the Shouter of the House. The legislature shall meet twenty-four hours a day with each of the three legislators from a town doing an eight-hour shift. (This will confuse lobbyists and so exhaust them that the people's business will be freed of their influence.)

Legislative Rules

- No legislator may abstain on a roll-call vote.
- No legislator may vote with his/her party more than sixty percent of the time.
- Yups and nopes will replace yeas and nays.
- Anyone caught sleeping or whispering during a debate will be immediately sent to the milkroom.[7]
- If the legislature adjourns for whatever reason at any hour of any day during the session, it shall be declared over.

[7] See page 138.

- Salaries shall be equal to Vermont's median weekly wage. They will be reduced by five percent each week of the session beyond March 1.

Qualifications for Election

- A person must survive six consecutive deer seasons in the same town or city before seeking election.
- All winners must take the following loyalty oath: "My loyalties are my own damned business."
- All legislators must know how to "rock" a car out of a snowbank, be capable of eating two servings of red flannel hash, and understand what it means to stand in line three hours to get a driver's license.

Powers of the Legislature

None. Except the following:

- The legislature may establish and maintain a list of official Vermont items such as the official state tree, vegetable, song, and the like.
- The legislature may lower taxes.
- The legislature may make all laws pertaining to the health and happiness of white-tailed deer.

That's all.

Session Length

In 1987 the Vermont legislature met until May 22, three weeks beyond schedule. Peas went unplanted. Spouses and voters chafed. One senator was so disgusted, she packed up and went home early. In 1988 the legislature didn't adjourn until June 14. In 1989 it met until July 4, when it adjourned out of respect for Senator Hughes Mudd, who disappeared after a raucous public meeting in Chester, where he had attempted to convince the Chamber of Commerce to outlaw yard sales.

In 1990 it continued until deer season. On November 20 Governor-elect Illusory, clad totally in red, charged onto the floor of the House, his hotseat flapping behind him, his earmuffs down, waving a rifle over his head. "Get the hell out of here! This is blasphemy!" he kept yelling. With every cry he fired a round into the ceiling. As the chamber emptied, he got off a "sound shot" at reporter Deborah Sline, who dived behind an antique spittoon. Then he charged the speaker's podium. But Speaker Ralph Wrong had made the right choice and left. Something had to be done.

The new Republic decided:

THE LEGISLATURE MAY MEET AS LONG AS IT WANTS TO, PROVIDED IT ADJOURNS BEFORE TOWN MEETING DAY.

Late on April 17, the last day of the constitutional convention, delegate Bill Mares left Montpelier with a copy of the new Constitution and headed home to Burlington. At the Waterbury exit he pulled off the interstate, turned onto Route 2, hooked a sharp right and immediately pulled to a stop at the pay phone in front of Hobbs Grocery. It was precisely 5:30. He got out of his car and dialed the same Washington, D.C., number that he had dialed every day at that time since TUGWOS.

On the third ring the call was answered, and a voice said, "There's good news and bad news. The bad news is that even though the Canaan fiasco shook Haig and popular opinion is now clearly on Vermont's side, he's not giving up. He's more determined than ever to bring you guys up there to heel. The good news is, he didn't fire McNearland, Poinsettia, and Bentley Bentley."

Mares smiled. At least the same bozos were still in the saddle. But Vermont's brief respite was obviously now over. Without a word he hung up, got back in his car, and drove west.

19

What to Do With Chittenden County?

April 19, 1991
(TUGWOS Plus 82)
The Abbey
Sheldon, Vermont

Maude Sodd of Sudbury was in a good mood. Today was her day to be Moderator of the Republic. And what a fine Republic it was! Yesterday the Town Meeting of the Republic had deftly handled a crisis at the Livingston Ski Area: a "meltdown" had occurred during the first heavy rain of the season. The manure bricks they'd used had turned the ski area into a manure pile. The problem had been solved by bulldozing the entire resort into the largest compost heap in the western hemisphere. There had also been a hot debate over whether listening to Lattie Coor give a speech should be a penalty for white-collar crime. But it was defeated as too severe. And finally, the new Solid Waste Disposal Act had been amended; it had not taken into account the environmental impact of burying Frank Bryan's obtuse books on Vermont politics.

The first item on the Warning today was a referendum on the location of the new national capital. Maude and husband Claude had drawn up the document the night before.

THE CAPITAL OF THE VERMONT REPUBLIC:
(VOTE FOR ONE)

_____ Shall remain in Montpelier, where it is now.

_____ Shall be moved to Windsor, where it first was.

_____ Shall be rotated from year to year from town to town, as it used to be.

_____ Shall be located permanently in Victory, where lobbyists would have trouble finding it.

_____ Shall be moved to Burlington, where no one would pay too much attention to it.

_____ Shall be moved to Halifax, because it's impossible to get there from anywhere.

_____ Shall be placed forever in Northfield. Northfield is perfect because

- It isn't shrouded by fog as much as Montpelier seems to be.
- It has no airport and would thus discourage too active a foreign policy.
- It is closer to the exact geographic center of the Republic.
- *Northfield* is more easily pronounced than *Montpelier,* which will help foreign journalists. It also sounds more like it's in Vermont—"north" and "field."

Maude wondered if listing all the reasons for Northfield— her particular favorite—unfairly biased the document. She concluded that if they didn't like it, they could TUGWOS.

"You have all had time to look it over?" she asked at the meeting. "May I have a motion to submit this referendum to the nation's voters?"

"So moved."

"Second?"

"Yup!"

"All those in fav—"

"Hey, how about some debate? Who drew this thing up?" asked someone.

"It was drawed by Maude 'n Claude."

"That's good 'nough for me."

"Those in favor?" asked Maude.

"The yups appear to have it. The yups *do* have it."

"Article Two," said Maude. "As you all know, the question of Chittenden County has been with us since long before TUGWOS. The problem came to a head in 1987, when it was announced that traffic reports would be made by air just as they are in New York City. Many folks said this was proof that Burlington had 'arrived.' Shoo!" said Maude, pausing briefly. "When traffic's so bad that airplanes have to tell people how to get to work, Burlington hasn't arrived — it's departed! It was at about that time, too, that those T-shirts began to appear saying, 'I like living in Chittenden County because it's so close to Vermont.' " There was general laughter. "Article Two on today's Warning is, 'What to do about Chittenden County?' What is your pleasure on Chittenden County?"

"Dig a ditch around it, float it across Lake Champlain, and attach it to New York State!" yelled Roy Titemore of Florence.

After the laughter subsided, Harlan Hancock of Wells rose stiffly from his chair. "Mrs. Moderator, I would like to place before this meeting the following resolution." He paused to clear his throat. "Keep Chittenden County, but require that each of its residents be recertified a Vermonter by checking in at certain locations outside Chittenden County at least once a year — places like Frank and Pierre's Steak House in Newport, Herb Ogden's cider mill in Hartland, the Tinmouth Public Library, the fish hatchery in Roxbury, the Blue Benn Diner in Bennington, and St. Albans City Hall."

After considerable discussion, Hancock's motion was defeated by a vote of 128 nopes to 115 yups. People in the spots Harlan mentioned feared an onslaught of flatlanders from Chittenden County. It just goes to show the new

Republic had not solved the NIMBY syndrome—Not In My Back Yard. Not *yet*!

The debate continued. Rob Cramer of Putney said, "It could be traded for Coös County, New Hampshire. We'd be swapping 115,534 people for 35,147, which may not seem like a good deal until you realize that one logger is worth six real estate dealers or seven UVM professors." This was defeated, 122 to 121.

Francine Lemieux of Bakersfield proposed, "Get everybody out, and then rent it to nations of the world as a site for training their street-fighting divisions. It could become the Fort Drum of city warfare. It's got everything: bridges, dams, beaches, railroads, tall buildings, underground sewers, a pedestrian mall with big boulders for machinegunners to hide behind. It has an airport to be taken, a TV station to be commandeered, a university where left-wingers could hole up. Competing blue and red squads could establish headquarters at Henry's and the Oasis Diners. It even has suburban sprawl and a rural/urban belt, which could be bombed by low-flying aircraft from Plattsburgh. We could rename the central city Beiruting-ton." This was defeated, 214 to 34.

David Switt of Thetford Center proposed, "Give the county two years to clean up its act, under threat of locking everyone in and making Bernard Sanders an absolute monarch for ten years." The meeting agreed that this was simply too harsh. It was defeated, 236 to 11.

Tom Reed of Wardsboro proposed, "Finish the Southern Connector, which will bring more traffic, so that more high-rise parking garages will be built, so that more stores will be piled in, so that more connectors will be constructed, so that more high-rises will rise higher, so that the lake and the sun will disappear from view, so that more legitimate excuses for driving the poor into trailer parks outside the city can be had, so that the poor can then use the connectors to drive in to clean the rooms and feed the tummies of the wealthy, so that more connectors will be needed and the present connectors can be widened and more cement poured and more sewage treated and more policemen hired to patrol the vast concrete deserts that the connectors surround and isolate." This, too, was defeated, 243 to 1.

Reginald Waterhouse of Shelburne proposed, "Leave it the way it is." This was defeated, 251 to 1.

Maude Sodd was depressed. It was lunchtime, but the issue still remained unresolved. She looked out at the crowd helplessly. "Well, I tried," she said.

"Don't worry about it, Maude!" yelled Lucien Chartier of Highgate Center. "We've been trying to figure out what to do with Chittenden County for fifty years! Hell, they don't even know themselves!"

Maude felt better. "It's about lunchtime. Bill?"

Mares stood up and the audience groaned. They sensed what was coming. "I don't like it any better than you do," he announced. "But two days ago, I learned that President Haig is hot after us again, despite what you read in the press." He looked at the front of the room and gave the "country music" signal to Norm Runnion. "There, now we're alone," he said as "My Heroes Have Always Been Cowboys" loudly traveled the airwaves from Sheldon to Washington, D.C. "Bentley Bentley has broken our code, and I don't know where the rascal is. In short, we've got to move again."

It was a worried Town Meeting of the Republic that filed out for lunch that day. If Bill Mares didn't know where Bentley Bentley was, who did?

20

The Capitol Building at Northfield

May 2, 1991
(TUGWOS Plus 95)

NORTHFIELD CHOSEN NATIONAL CAPITAL read the headlines of the Republic's newspapers on May 2, 1991. "Maude Sodd of Sudbury announced today that the people of Vermont have voted to move the government 'more toward the exact center of the country.' According to Mrs. Sodd, the following decisions have also been made regarding a new capitol building. Ben Mason will next Friday supervise the helicopter transport of the old Delbert Leete Round Barn in Newbury to Northfield. It will be redesigned as the new State House.

"Mrs. Sodd also announced that the redesign of the building has been completed. Highlights:

- The main feature is a single, huge, round legislative chamber. Lawmakers sit in the stalls circling the interior of the room. This emphasizes their equality.
- The Shouter's podium is situated in the exact center of the chamber on a wagon of loosely baled hay.[1] During the sessions, the wagon will be rotated very slowly by a pair of oxen so that the Shouter can see each legislator.

[1] The poor footing will keep him awake.

Gavels don't work on hay, so the Shouter tinkles the session to order with a cowbell.

- The office of the Moderator of the Republic is in the silo just outside the barn. In accordance with the separation of powers principle, the Moderator is prohibited from entering the barn through the main doors but comes through the milkroom, now a sergeant-at-arms office.
- The entire national bureaucracy is located above the legislature in the hayloft. When legislators wish to question an agency head, that person is dropped through a hay chute into the center of the barn to face a circle of legislators, neatly positioned in their stalls.
- The statue of Ceres, the goddess of agriculture, is to be removed from the old capitol in Montpelier and placed atop the round barn, where it will be more at home. Ethan Allen's assertive figure, too, will travel south to guard the milkroom door."

21

Vermont National Holidays

May 22, 1991
(TUGWOS Plus 115)
Bennington, Vermont

It was a beautiful spring day. The lilacs were between bud and blossom, the dandelions a million gold-drops in the green, and the deep blue sky was a playground where the breeze played tag with great, rolling fluffs of cotton. Everywhere the citizens of Vermont were in a festive mood. The corn was planted. The hay was almost ready. The international community seemed to have accepted Vermont. Trade was increasing. Best of all, FUS had made no moves against the Republic for some time. It seemed that moving the Town Meeting of the Republic from town to town was keeping Bentley Bentley at bay.

That week the Town Meeting had been moved to Bennington for the week. The afternoon session was held outdoors on the grounds of the Bennington Battle Monument. People sat on blankets or in folding chairs, while children romped and dogs barked. The Moderator stood on a platform before the Monument and used a microphone, for the crowd was swelled by foreign dignitaries, tourists, and schoolchildren. A half-dozen people roamed the audience with portable microphones.

Justin Willey of Pownal called the meeting to order.

"Whatta we do with the flatlanders?" somebody yelled. "They can't vote, can they?

"Give me that microphone," said Calvin Proctor of Jamaica. "Visitors have always been allowed to sneak in a vote or two at town meeting," he reminded the crowd. "Let's not worry about it unless they get outta hand. I make that a motion!"

"All those in favor?" asked Justin.

"Wait." Frank Bryan leaped to his feet; sitting next to him, Bill Mares covered his face. "Nobody seconded the motion!"

"Yup!" came the thunderous vote of the throng. Even a few dogs yelped their enthusiasm.

"All those opposed?"

"Nope," muttered Bryan to himself, sinking onto his blanket.

"Befitting this beautiful afternoon," Moderator Willey told the crowd, "the first order of business and the *only* order of business" — shouts of agreement — "will be the approval of the list of proposed National Holidays for the Republic." (General applause.) "It is my pleasure to introduce to you Ms. Geraldine Jacobs of Rupert, chairperson of the Holiday Committee." (More applause.)

"Ladies and gentlemen," began Geraldine, "all work and no play makes nations dull, too. Vermonters are known for their hard work, but they enjoy time off as much as anyone." She paused to let the cheering subside. "Your committee has decided to propose several new holidays for Vermont." She began to read:

February 2: Groundhog Day

Another name for groundhog is woodchuck. Need we say more? Vermont will celebrate Groundhog Day as a National Holiday. Only here it will be called Woodchuck Day.

January 27: Secession Day

The memory of the glorious day when Vermont flung open her doors and tossed out "the other forty-nine" will be celebrated throughout the state. Symbolic cardboard bridges will be blown up, and zucchini contests for schoolchildren will be held; in them, frozen squash will be rolled down hillsides toward targets at the bottom.

Any Day You Want Day

Every Vermonter will be allowed to excuse himself or herself one day a year to celebrate Ethan Allen's birthday. Since no one knows the exact date of his birth, Vermonters will pick their own days. Ethan would have liked it that way.

November 4: Flood Day

This day will memorialize the Great Flood of 1927 and Vermont's subsequent dual act of independence and wisdom; independence in refusing help from Washington and cleaning up the mess itself; and wisdom for quietly pocketing it when later Washington did slip a few bucks Vermont's way.

The First Tuesday of March: Town Meeting Day

It's about time we let working people in on our democracy. If people go ice fishing or snowmobiling or sugar-making on Town Meeting Day, so be it.

October 6: Old Home Day

Around the turn of the twentieth century, the Vermont legislature brazenly stole the idea of Old Home Week from New Hampshire. Old Home Week soon became Old Home Day. (A week was a bit much, even for civic-spirited New Englanders.) This event drew natives back to Vermont from throughout the world to celebrate town life. The Republic will set off one day each year — October 6[1] — to do the same.

"Now," continued Geraldine, "in addition to these six new National Holidays, we have holidays left over from our association with FUS."

Labor Day

Labor Day will be retained as a day for working, not sitting around. On Labor Day, every citizen must report to the town hall to work on some mutually acceptable public-service project. Labor Day will be postponed until the third Monday in September to insure that there will be enough cider to get us through the day.

Veterans Day

Vermont will join FUS to honor the men and women who kept us safe and free for two hundred years.

Presidents' Day

Here's an example of why we got out. It was an unholy union of separate events, united by the fast lane and the three-day weekend. Let's bag it.

Martin Luther King Day

It remains.

Thanksgiving

It too remains. However, venison and wild turkey will be added to the traditional fare again. Anyone caught watching a football game instead of being outside working

[1] Unless individual towns decide to hold it on some other day, which is, of course, their right.

up an appetite will be condemned to have the following sign painted on the house:

HEREIN LIVES A COUCH POTATO. HONK IF YOU AGREE.

The Fourth of July

Vermont will still honor FUS's Independence Day. We had more to do with it than anyone else.

Christmas

Christmas will still be Christmas. We know it isn't exactly fair to single out the Christian religion. But the Republic of Vermont doesn't claim to be perfect.[2]

"We also suggest that we hold an essay contest in the high schools now and then to determine if another National Holiday is needed. Suggestions for the next one are:"

Tow Day

To celebrate the opening of the first ski tow in Woodstock, or the great blizzard of 1969. Take your pick.

Flake Day

To celebrate the first time Snowflake Bentley photographed a snowflake, or Jim Jeffords's birthday. Take your pick.

Sap Day

To celebrate the first day sap flows in any given year, or the first time you outfoxed a flatlander. Take your pick.

---

[2] It *will* be law in Vermont that any religious group can use public facilities to celebrate its holy days if one-tenth of one percent of the voters agree.

"Your committee thanks you for your kind attention," said Geraldine Jacobs of Rupert, handing the microphone back to Moderator Justin Willey as the crowd applauded.

Thirty seconds later the list was approved.

"Before we adjourn," yelled Justin into the microphone, "before we adjourn . . ." The audience groaned. They had heard the one phrase town meeting–goers dread the most, the old "before we adjourn" ploy.

"I have some announcements to make. This evening there will be a band concert here on the grounds. Tomorrow, the town of Woodford's Ladies' Aid Society is holding their annual bake sale on the village green, and the children of Wilmington Grade School will present their annual spring play, this year an original adaptation of *Anne of Green Gables.*"

As the crowd dispersed, two figures remained seated.

"Stop blubbering!" hissed Mares.

"I can't help it," sobbed Bryan, his head bowed into clenched fists, wet and grimy with tears. "It's so damned *beautiful,* Bill. Bake sales, band concerts, little girls playing Anne of Green Gables. This is how it's *supposed* to be!" He sobbed again. "I'm just so happy!"

"Something in his eye," Mares explained to a passerby.

Hundreds of miles to the south in Washington, D.C., it was hot and humid. In his air-conditioned office in the cellar of the White House, Bentley Bentley sat reading still another folder of press clippings on Vermont. Suddenly he stopped reading and stared at the page before him. Then, hands trembling with excitement, he pushed the buzzer on his desk. "Get McNearland and Poinsettia in here, *now!*"

"But sir, they're shredding."

"Now, or I'll shred you!"

"Yes, sir."

"Gentlemen," said Bentley after they arrived a few minutes later, "look at this." He showed them an article on town meeting published in a Vermont newspaper in the 1980s. In it, Charles Kurault, CBS's famous *On the Road* reporter, was quoted as saying that of all the places he'd visited across America, the one he liked best and remembers the most was "South Strafford, Vermont, on Town Meeting Day."

Bentley lowered his voice to a whisper. "Don't you see? This place, South Strafford, has what Bryan himself calls the quintessential town meeting place—a meeting house on a knoll in South Strafford Village. Look at this." He referred to the ten-by-twenty-foot relief map of Vermont that dominated the situation room. "These places are where they've held their meetings before," he said, his voice rising in excitement. "And gentlemen, right in the middle of the sector where no meetings have been held to date, is South Strafford, Vermont, the 'quintessential' meeting place!"

Poinsettia and McNearland looked confused.

"Dummies!" screamed Bentley Bentley. "Don't you see? Sooner or later they'll show up in South Strafford! All we have to do is get there first and lay for 'em."

"Ah," said his two assistants.

"Now. Get me a thousand of our best troops—none from states like Texas or Montana or Alaska or Wyoming. We can't afford any defections. Understood?"

"Yes, sir!"

Bentley Bentley rubbed his hands together. Yes, indeed, sooner or later Vermont's government would end up in South Strafford. And when it did . . . oh, the joy of it!

22

Making Do
the High-Tech Way

June 6, 1991
(TUGWOS Plus 131)
Montpelier, Vermont

The Provisional Government met for the first time in the former State House. Using the Town Meeting of the Republic format as usual, it elected former State Senator Bill Doyle as Moderator. He immediately called Article 1, a proposal to get Vermont into the jail business. "The chair recognizes David Hale of St. Johnsbury," he said.

"Hey, he ain't no citizen no more! Don't he live out there in Chicago or one of them other cities on the West Coast?" It was Walter Wheeler of Chelsea.

"Oh, for god's sake, shut up, Walter!" yelled his neighbor and fifth cousin, Walter Wheeler of Chelsea, from the gallery. "Don't you know *he's the patron saint of Vermont Secession*?"

"Wal, all right, then."

Hale began, "Thank you for having me. It is true I live in Chicago, but my heart will always be in Vermont." (Applause.) "Your economy is quite strong, as you know, but in the long haul you will have to be more and more imaginative and adjust the concept of 'making do' to the world of high technology.

"Why not make Vermont a penal colony for high-tech criminals?" he said. There were gasps from the audience.

In the gallery mothers clutched their children to their
bosoms. "No—hear me out," said Hale with a grin.
"Instead of soliciting captive insurance companies and
financial service firms, Vermont should capitalize on the
growing number of 'captive' or convicted investment
bankers by converting one of its under-used ski areas into a
low-security prison. Such prisons typically offer a wide
range of amenities, such as golf courses, libraries, and
gymnasiums, so they would be a logical extension of the
tourist business.

"Moreover, this would accelerate your campaign to
attract more Japanese investment. It is well known that
Japanese brokerage houses regularly engage in insider trad-
ing. Hence, with the growing Japanese presence in the New
York financial community, there are likely to be hundreds
of Japanese brokers heading for U.S. prisons. If they serve
terms in Vermont and enjoy the experience, it could
improve the Republic's business image.

"Most important, the Republic of Vermont's low-security
prison could be used for wayward investment bankers from
around the world. Many European countries have offshore
penal colonies—that's why Australia was founded. So
perhaps we should establish a treaty with FUS whereby
Vermont would serve as a penal colony for Wall Street.

"And why not? So what if some fat cat from the SEC or
the London Stock Exchange or a West German investment
company 'escapes' from this 'prison'? Where would they
go? It would be like Devil's Island or Alcatraz. Instead of
dying in shark-filled waters, they would risk being run
down by a snowmobiler or mistaken for a deer by a hunter
as they wandered through the forests of Vermont. What
harm would occur if they did 'escape'? Would they
commandeer an IBM PC and infiltrate our new passport
market? Would they sneak into a schoolyard and fill children's minds with evil ways of buying on the margin or
leaking information about the futures market?

"Come on! They're harmless. Let them be jailed in
Vermont, where they can ski and sauna and play tennis to

their hearts' content. Governing elites of the sending nations will *want* these privileged white-collar, high-tech criminals to have a good time, since they realize they may end up incarcerated in Vermont themselves someday. Heck, all we'll have to do is to take down a sign like 'Hog Mountain North Ski Area' and replace it with 'Hog Mountain International Penal Resort for the Marginally Guilty.' "

The debate began. After several hours of give and take, his proposal was approved by a vote of 181 yups to 162 nopes.

That afternoon, Doyle recognized Walter Wheeler of Washington first.

"I've got an idea," said the cousin of the Chelsea Wheelers.

"Cousin Walter looks good this summer, don't he?" said Walter Wheeler of Chelsea to his new seatmate, Walter Wheeler of Chelsea, who had moved down from the gallery.

Walter began, "There's money in morality!" (Dead silence.) "Let me tell you what I mean. The United States is going through a moral breakdown that recalls the depravity of the Roman Empire. On Wall Street, the Ivan Boeskys steal millions. Business schools offer courses in ethics—as an elective! Making deals is better than making a decent product. Greed is hallowed above all. Christmas is just another gimmick to boost slow fourth-quarter GNP figures."

"That's the truth!" shouted Walter Wheeler of Chelsea.

"Where will it all end?" asked Walter. "No one knows." He paused for effect, the Yankee in him forming beads of sweat on his brow. "But I'll tell you one thing—Vermont can *cash in* on it. We can offer Americans a place to get away and restore their ethical roots. We can provide a dozen or so 'Vermont-Is-What-America-Was' Honesty, Humility and Charity Fitness Centers!

"In places like Calais, Pittsford, Bristol, and Wilmington, helpful staffs will design individually tailored programs in moral isometrics. Guests will squirm in whirlpools of humility and sweat in saunas of justice.

"That's not all. Each morning and afternoon the staff will lead mandatory sessions at the resort woodpile, sledge-hammer work in the granite shed, and shoveling manure on the resort farm. They'll be given work as busboys or chambermaids. They'll suffer insults and ridicule. Don't you see?" said Wheeler with a sly grin. "They'll *love* it.

"Every culture needs someone to look down upon. Since everyone is equal in Vermont, we'll be importing our own 'underclass'! We'll also give the guests a chance to stand on the bottom rung for a change. Imagine how good they'll feel being demoted, demeaned, and derided in the morning and safe in the afternoon or evening, back among their own kind at the Center.

"They can be sent on field trips into town to see ordinary people being kind to each other. They'll watch and practice spontaneous smiling. They'll learn how to admit a mistake—and mean it. I'm telling you, my friends." Walter Wheeler was by now enthusiastic. "Americans are so guilt-ridden, they'll flock to Vermont to be cleansed. They'll spend millions here! Believe me, Vermonters, this one's a winner." He sat down.

Doyle approached the podium.

"Call the question," came a shout from the audience.

"All those in favor of suspending debate and voting immediately on the motion to appropriate fifty thousand dollars to help promote these Centers in Vermont, say yup," said Doyle.

Everyone said yup. My God, thought Wheeler, they're going to do it without debate. All right!

"All those in favor of the motion, signify by saying yup."

"Yup," said the Walter Wheelers of Chelsea.

"Against?"

"Nope," said everyone else.

"Crimus," said the Walter Wheelers of Chelsea.

"Mr. Moderator." It was Bill Mares.

"Have we gotta move *again*?"

"I'm afraid so," said Mares. "Frank Bryan, who would have been here but his truck broke down, has suggested South Strafford."

Later that evening Bill Mares picked up the phone at the booth in Waterbury and punched in the number. He listened intently for several minutes and then hung up without saying a word. Where was Bentley Bentley? Two weeks ago he'd dropped out of sight. Mares didn't like it. He didn't like it at all.

23

The Thistle Doctrine

Vermont's Foreign Policy
June 12, 1991
(TUGWOS) Plus 137)
The Meeting House
South Strafford, Vermont

High on a hill in the woods above South Strafford,
Lieutenant Colonel Bentley Bentley stared through a small
telescope at the village below. It was 2:50 P.M. He and his
troops had been lying in wait for the Republic's Provisional
Government for two weeks, and they looked it.

"When are we going to strike, colonel?" asked one of his
lieutenants, slapping at another mosquito. "Look at the
size of that one!" he exclaimed to a private beside him. "I
heard they named the mosquito the national bird."

Nobody laughed.

Bentley scanned the surrounding hills. All units were in
place. One thousand crack FUS commandos stood ready to
swarm the tiny village. By his count, there were only 236
people inside the Meeting House. "Let's give them another
half-hour," he said. "So far, Mares hasn't shown up, and
I'd like to get him, too. Know something else? There are a
lot of foreign reporters down there. What luck! They'll all
get to witness the end of the Republic of Vermont."

Meanwhile, inside the South Strafford Meeting House,
line-by-line editing of the document outlining Vermont's
foreign policy had been in progress since nine that morning. Vermont's re-won independence had attracted the

attention of the world's press. It was akin to Siberia lifting its leg on the Soviet Union, Buda dropping Pest, Barnum quitting Bailey.

To go it alone, Vermont needed an effective foreign policy. Drawing on historical precedents, Vermont had issued its first foreign policy declaration within forty-eight hours of the end of TUGWOS. Known as the Thistle Doctrine, it was simplicity itself:

WE AIN'T WORTH THE TROUBLE WE CAN CAUSE.

No one should have been surprised at Vermont's sophistication. After all, the world's first globes were manufactured in Bradford, and the first ambassador to the United Nations, Warren Austin, was a Vermonter.

Since the early days a committee had been drafting the Thistle Doctrine even as the Republic was putting it in practice. On June 9, 1991, in the South Strafford Meeting House, a final draft was distributed, and the Moderator of the Republic, Lillian Little of Irasburg, had gaveled the meeting to order at 9:15.

"The only article on the Republic's Warning today," she said, "is consideration of the Thistle Doctrine. I will now call upon Emory Hebard, chairman of the committee that drafted the document, to read it, prior to our section-by-section discussion of it. Em?"

"Thank you, Mrs. Moderator. Let me begin."

THE THISTLE DOCTRINE

Preamble

"Never Get Into a Pissin' Contest With a Skunk."

Foreign Alliances

The new Republic of Vermont is a friend to every nation on earth, except those we don't like. We believe in the Vermont proverbs, "Give neither salt nor counsel until asked for it," and, "Don't be dipping your lip in another's porridge."[1] We intend to be forever neutral in the squabbles of the world, unless we decide not to be. The only exception is our defense pact with FUS. We unilaterally decided to come to its aid if it is attacked by anyone. This is a perpetual agreement that we will adhere to forever unless we decide not to.

We will not join NATO because we have no coastline on the Northern Atlantic (although many Vermont eels go there to make love). We won't join SEATO since we don't know what it means.

Vermont will be *especially* neutral if Zaire attacks Tanzania, Bolivia invades Algeria, Uzbekistan swallows Kazakhstan, or Texas joins Mexico.

United Nations Policy

The Republic of Vermont will seek membership in the United Nations. Although we are new and small, we do not consider ourselves a First, Second, or Third World nation.

We are a Fourth World nation.

As our interim ambassador to the United Nations, Ralph Wrong, said in his maiden speech, the Fourth World nations represent a group of independent states who are strategically located thorns in superpower flesh—nations such as Albania, Afghanistan, Finland, Mongolia, Greece,

[1] From Wolfgang Mieder's *Talk Less and Say More.*

and New Zealand. "Together we will seek power through our capacity to annoy, annoy, annoy, annoy. We will," said Wrong, "pain Spain, hiss the Swiss, irk the Turk, and bait Kuwait. We will pique Peking and mock Mexico. We'll even annoy Hanoi. Power to pipsqueaks. Common to all Fourth World nations is a willingness and a history of saying to a superpower, 'Stick it in *your* ear!' "

Defense Policy

Vermont's first line of defense is to become an indispensable element of the peace process itself. On the premise that it would be dastardly to trash a seat of international negotiations, Vermont will become the new Geneva of the world.

- A Chair of Conflict Resolution is created in the political science department at the University of Vermont.[2]
- Johnson National College will become the world's first college completely devoted to peace studies, offering a single degree, the Bachelor of Getting Along.
- An Aiken Corps has been formed that will seek peace aggressively with advice like "Everyone declare themselves a victor and go home." It will show up in hostile areas, its members in bib overalls and straw hats chewing on timothy grass. Using key negotiating terms like *yup, nope, 'pears to be,* and *'bout right,* the Vermonters will shame international combatants into peace by demonstrating a common-sensical awareness that we're all in this together. If this fails, the Aiken Corps will become like Edward Abbey's Monkeywrench Gang, sending illicit peace messages to warring factions, causing peaceful signs and signals to appear along tense international borderlines, kidnapping warring elites on both sides of disputes, and forcing them to sit on stools naked and look each other in the eye until they start to giggle.
- Vermont will offer the United Nations its own Camp David, where delegations can come for rest and relaxa-

[2] Once the chair has been built, it is hoped that a fund can be established to hire a professor to fill it.

tion. Instead of traffic, pollution, and crime, Vermont will offer the nations of the world fresh air and a slow, *peaceful* life-style. Nations that play together, stay together.

Vermont's second line of defense is to become a permanent home for the Olympic Games. Training sites for the games will be open year-round to all nations. Thus, states like Egypt and Chad and Fiji, which don't have snow, can use the Olympic facilities here. The purpose is not so much economic gain as the idea that at any given time an attack on Vermont will involve great risk to heroes from many of the world's nations. We will be able to say, "Shoot, and you may wipe out the Albanian soccer team," or, "Don't forget, the Russian women's shotput team is training in Granby!" or, "Drop one on Rutland, and you'll vaporize the Italian water polo team at the Holiday Inn."

If all this fails, Vermont's third line of defense will be, regrettably, military action.

At that point Em Hebard was interrupted. "Never!" cried Mavin Pugh of Pownal. "Let's disarm completely, utterly, finally!" The director of Convenience Store Owners for Social Responsibility continued, "We led the way with the nuclear freeze in 1982. We can lead the way in 1992!"

"Gutless pacifists!" scorned "Tater" Robinson, a retired railway worker from Maidstone. "Let's get FUS to put their MX missiles in Vermont. We got hundreds of miles of abandoned railroad tracks. That'll keep them Russkies at bay!"

"Sure," cried Hercule Noel of Cambridge. "That's all I need! To wake up in the morning and have a six-story MX missile inching by the house on the Lamoille Valley Railroad. Are you out of your mind, Tater?"

"Enough!" It was Madeline Harwood, flanked by Peter Diamondstone. She brought the gavel crashing down. Dead silence struck the South Strafford Meeting House, and Em Hebard continued reading:

- We have already nationalized General Electric's Gatling Gun plant in Burlington, the largest factory building these weapons in the world. Even Rambo's eyes gleam when he sees six thousand rounds a minute spurt from their barrels.
- Our snowmobile fleet is the largest in the world and operated by the most skillful riders. Attack Vermont in winter, and you've had it.
- Gliders from Warren provide us with a strike force that can sweep silently out of Vermont skies to strike targets well beyond our own borders.
- The Vermont Federation of Outdoor Sportsmen (already armed to the teeth with high-powered rifles equipped with scopes) has been formed into a twenty-five-thousand-person Sniper Division. Trained to bring down a running white-tail in heavy brush at one hundred yards while sitting in a tree holding on with one hand and gripping a flask of Canadian Velvet between their teeth, these hunters can do the same from the front seat of a '72 Ford cruising in heavy traffic at 65 miles per hour on the interstate or bouncing down a country road in the backseat of a '68 Chevy.

  These men and women are used to long hours in the cold, sitting motionless on their "stand" while their fingers and toes become as one and the minutes drag on like Sunday afternoons. Bring on the Green Berets! There is no training as harsh as hunting in Vermont. They know the countryside like the back of their hands. Woe to any foreign troops who venture onto our hills to do battle with these shadowy denizens of the forest deep!

It was 2:50 in the afternoon before the final tally was taken on the Thistle Doctrine. Thirty-six individual votes had preceded final approval—a unanimous yup. The cheers of foreign newsmen were heard live over WFREE.

Following this, a series of routine announcements was read by Philip Hoff, chairman of Vermont's Interim Foreign Policy Council.

- All nations needing lots for their embassies in the capital at Northfield should apply for Act 250 permits immediately. There are 224 different stops to be made before a permit to apply for a permit is permitted.
- In reply to the Soviet Union's offer to allow us to use an embassy building in Moscow abandoned in 1987 by the United States: we accept gratefully, even though we know it's bugged. Frankly, we don't give a hoot how much you listen to us. You'll find that we have damned little to say.
- Message to New Hampshire: Same to you, Bucko.

At this point Bill Mares walked into the back of the South Strafford Meeting Hall. It was 3:10. He'd had a tough day and was upset he'd missed the vote on the Thistle Doctrine. But he felt something else, too, a nagging uncertainty, like when you leave home on an important trip feeling you've forgotten something. His mind was thus occupied as the reading of the foreign policy announcements continued.

- Milton Friedman, who had been vacationing in Vermont during TUGWOS, has agreed to become our ambassador to Hong Kong. Richard Snelling was offered the ambassadorship to either Graustark or Ruritania. Other ambassadorships:
  a. John Murphy of Ludlow is ambassador to Ireland.
  b. Howard Dean is ambassador to somewhere. He says he doesn't care what office he holds as long as he's appointed to something.
  c. Peter Welch is ambassador to Nauru. He'll leave as soon as we can find an airline that goes there.
- We have signed an agreement with the nation of Oman and several lesser Trucial sheikdoms to exchange oil for water. For every barrel of oil shipped to Vermont, we will clean the barrel and return it filled with pure spring water. This agreement opens the spigot for the Vermont water industry in the Persian Gulf. We led the old

United States in the returnable bottle policy; now we'll lead the world in returnable barrels.

- We wish to thank Commandante Daniel Ortega of Nicaragua for his gift. Unfortunately, the banana trees arrived on February 18 frozen solid, even though the temperature had risen to minus six degrees. The Russian hats and mittens were most welcome, however.
- Thanks but no thanks to Imelda Marcos for her donation of 3,000 pairs of shoes—not one of them would keep out rain, let alone snow.
- Message to Secretary Gorbachev: The janitorial staff of FUS's embassy in Northfield has already been hired.

Either by luck or by some other unfathomable explanation, a cluster of brain waves in Bill Mares's agile mind suddenly snapped into alignment. The mention of Gorbachev had reminded him of war, and war had reminded him of the military, and the military, of his marine training: "Find a place where sooner or later you know they'll be, and then go there and wait—wait for as long as it takes."

What was it Bryan had said last night? "Sorry I can't make it tomorrow, Bill. South Strafford's town meeting hall is world famous. Anyone who knows Vermont knows that sooner or later we'd hold a meeting there, but I gotta teach!" Mares's mind raced on. Bentley Bentley was a marine! Bentley Bentley had read everything ever written about Vermont! It was 3:15.

A cold hand descended on Mares's neck. Oh m'god, those silver speckles in the trees above town . . . those daylight fireflies in the sun. He whirled and burst out the door. The brightness blinded him. But it didn't matter.

"Good afternoon, Mares." Bentley Bentley smiled. "They told me you were smarter than this."

24

Madeline Has Her Say

June 14, 1991
(TUGWOS Plus 139)
The White House
Washington, D.C.

With the 237-person government of the Republic of Vermont in Washington under lock and key at the marine barracks at Eighth and "I" Streets, Lieutenant Colonel Bentley Bentley, USMC, allowed himself a breath of relief. Sitting beside the President in the Oval Office, he tried not to gloat as McNearland and Poinsettia ushered Harwood, Bryan, and Mares into the room.

President Haig got right to business. He had to. International support for Vermont was vocal and growing. The UN Security Council was holding an emergency session that morning. FUS embassies in Switzerland, Uruguay, and Monaco were besieged by protesters. Two correspondents for The Movie Channel and Home Box Office had been kidnapped in Lebanon by the Hezbollah, which offered to exchange their freedom for Vermont's. Thank God, he sighed to himself, no one had been killed up at Strafford and there was only one injury.

In fact, Haig mused further, it was downright odd how complacent the government of Vermont had been. Their vaunted Hill Farmer Brigade never showed. No one in South Strafford had been armed. The only resistance to capture had come from that maniac Bryan. That was why

Haig's first question to Bentley over the radio as the commandos headed back to Washington, D.C., had been, "Are you *sure* these are Vermonters? If this is another Dixville Notch . . ."

"Don't sweat it, Mr. President, we're cool," Bentley had replied.

Turning to the respectful yet queerly self-assured prisoners, Haig said, "I have a document of surrender for the State of Vermont. All it means is that you will return to the status quo ante, before you so imprudently left the Union."

"TUGWOS!" said Mares.

"Beg your pardon?" Haig replied.

"TUGWOS, *sir!*" repeated Bryan.

Harwood giggled. "Now, boys."

Haig shook his head. He continued, "Before the cameras arrive for the signing ceremony, I have one question."

"Yes, Mr. President?" said Madeline Harwood.

"Why did you do it?"

"You remember what J. P. Morgan supposedly said — 'If you have to ask what a yacht costs, you probably can't afford to buy one'? Same thing here. If you have to ask, you probably can't understand the answer."

"Come on, Madeline, let's tell him anyway," said Bryan. "It's like Ethan Allen said: 'The gods of the hills are not the gods of the valleys.' "

Like a boxer who had gone one too many rounds, Haig again shook his head. But he kept his composure; after all, he did have the entire government in his clutches.

"So," he said grandly, "let's get on with the show. Madeline — I can call you Madeline, can't I?"

"Why, of course, Alexander."

"When the TV camera crews come in, I'll simply read this document that you've already seen and then ask you to sign it. You'll sign here and here." Haig leaned across the table, pointing carefully to two Xs on the document.

"Oh my, Alex," said Madeline innocently. "We can't sign those papers."

"Why not?" asked Haig, sitting back, genuinely surprised.

"Because we aren't the government of Vermont."

"What?" Haig cast a quick glance at Bentley Bentley,
who turned white.

"Oh, no," said Madeline, catching Haig's look, "it isn't
his fault. We *were* the government when he captured us."

"Mrs. Harwood," said Alexander Haig, President of
FUS. "I'm a reasonable man. Will you please explain?"

"Why, Alex, I thought you knew. I thought everyone
knew. *In Vermont, the government's everyone.* If you want
to kidnap the government, *you'll have to catch us all,* and
we have at least 300,000 registered voters.

"You see, Alex, at this very moment the government of
Vermont is meeting. All you have here are 237 citizens who
happened to attend the Town Meeting of the Republic that
day."

Bentley Bentley leaped to his feet, stared murderously at
Harwood for an instant, and then headed for the basement
to check his radio.

"But how can that be?" yelled the President of FUS.
"We have the government here. *You* are the government.
We've cut the head off the body of state."

"No—" began Madeline, but Haig interrupted.

"Everyone can't govern. Ordinary people aren't capable.
They're not *trained!*"

"Oh, yes they are," Harwood continued. "It's our town
meeting tradition. In Vermont every citizen is a legislator.
Everyone learns how to govern. It's as natural as learning
how to walk. That's why we hold on to our town meetings,
Mr. President. You see, Alex"—she lowered her voice and
leaned toward him across the desk, nodding affirmatively—
*"in Vermont everyone is equal. The government is all of
us."*

"You mean . . . " said Haig, aghast.

"Yessir." Madeline leaned back in her chair, beaming.

"Really?"

"Yes."

"You have a . . . "

"Say it, Mr. President—a de- . . . "

"A democracy," stammered the President of the Former United States, half in disbelief, half in awe.

"Bingo!" said Mares.

Deep in the basement of the White House, Bentley Bentley sat transfixed before his radio. From the Green Mountains far to the north came the voice of Norm Runnion: "Good morning, fellow Vermonters. I'm here at the auction barn in Morrisville, where today's session of the Town Meeting of the Republic is about to get under way. Theron Cote of Orleans has been chosen Moderator of the Republic. . ."

25

Red Dawn Over the Kingdom

August 5, 1991
(TUGWOS Plus 190)
South America Pond, Vermont

It snaked out through the wisp of mist that hovered just above the water, cutting the pink glow of dawn in a long, silent arc. Pausing ever so slightly between the two horizons, it settled quietly onto the dark glass at the precise spot where the mountains of the Northeast Kingdom met themselves on the face of the lake. Bill watched the tiny ripple play itself out until the mirror was pure again. Then, slowly, carefully, he began to inch the Hornberg toward himself. The planet was perfectly still. Only a hint of chill foreshadowed the deep cold of winter already gathering in the north.

It had been good, the trip up to South America Pond the day before. He and Bryan had reminisced about the eventful days following the beginning of TUGWOS on January 27, which seemed a lifetime ago: the revolution's early success, the long weeks of playing cat and mouse with FUS, the ups and downs, the growing excitement of success, and the depression that followed the "massacre"— Bill still liked to call it that—at Strafford.

They laughed over Bryan's attempt to ram Bentley Bentley's helicopter with his GMC. The same premonition that had hit Mares in the South Strafford Meeting House had struck Bryan during his Vermont politics class at UVM. Forgetting to call ahead, he arrived at South Strafford just as Bentley's copter was rising from the ground. But the engine exploded just before he reached the copter, leaving him ten feet short. "I'm always too short!" screamed a maddened Bryan as he leaped from the truck and kicked it, breaking his little toe and becoming the only casualty of the South Strafford Massacre.

Finally they shared once again the memory of that glorious day only a week later when President Haig had finally given up—the sound and passion of the procession up I-91 through Massachusetts to Vermont as a delegation from FUS marched north to sign the peace treaty. The Haig motorcade had led an ever-growing caravan of well-

wishers as it traveled north through New England. There under the old "Unwelcome to Vermont" sign on the (now defunct) northbound lane of I-91, Haig had signed the mutual defense treaty that Vermont's Danny Gore had drawn up the night before. It was a good one, a one-liner:

GOOD FENCES MAKE GOOD NEIGHBORS.

What a happy occasion it had been! Lieutenant Colonel Bentley Bentley had been left in Washington. Haig seemed honestly friendly.[1] Hundreds of thousands of liberty lovers from all over the world were present. Bands played.

Mares looked up at the mountains and breathed a long sigh of relief, his hands at rest, his flyline slack, his mind caught up in the deep quiet of dawn.

Suddenly a loud *ker-splash* ruined everything. It was Bryan. Mares looked to his right. An orange bobber the size of a softball popped up and down in the swells caused by its own crash landing. Then came another loud splash, and another bobber hit the water to his left. Bill whirled around just as Bryan was winding up with his third. Bill ducked as it came whistling—three heavily wormed hooks trailing behind—out over his head and splashed into the pond.

"You wanna play games or catch some fish?" yelled Bryan just before he lost his footing on the muddy bank and fell over backward. "Sheet!" he said disgustedly.

Mares grinned. What the hell? He hadn't come to South America Pond to flyfish anyway, not really. He headed back to camp to start breakfast, and by 7:30 (Bryan had actually caught some pan fries) they were relaxed and happy.

Meanwhile it had been a typical morning in the White House basement. President Haig finished working out on the heavy bag and went for a swim. In the Situation Room

---

[1] He had consoled himself that at least the American flag would look more symmetrical with Vermont gone—seven rows and seven columns of stars.

the teletypes chattered out their daily recital of natural and manmade disasters. A bus bombing in Sri Lanka, a typhoon in Okinawa, an oil tanker sinking in the English Channel, Vanna White defecting to the new *Hollywood Squares*—it was a normal day. The White House staff saw no need to disturb the President.

At about 11:30, Lieutenant Colonel Bentley Bentley, coffee cup in hand, made his way past the two sleeping marine guards and walked over to the Associated Press wires. He read a dateline—Helena, Montana. "Truck drivers and waitresses have occupied Molly's Truck Stop on I-15 five miles south of here and have declared Montana an independent nation. . . ."

"What the hell?" gasped Bentley. Could it be that his worst fears were coming to pass?

As he watched, the AP moved to a second story. This one had a *flash*. The truck-stop rebellion had spread into the streets of Helena, and gangs of cowboys and schoolchildren were blocking Interstate 15 and passing out flags and flowers to those who would join. Out-of-staters were allowed to continue their journey, but Montana residents were signing oaths of allegiance as fast as they could be printed.

Bentley rushed to a chartreuse phone and dialed twenty-seven digits. The voice that answered at the other end of the line was close to panic. "All hell's broken loose here! We've got truckers, cowboys, school kids, mothers, street crews, and bankers. They've come out onto the streets and are shouting and demonstrating that they've had it up to their kiesters with the federal government! They're screaming about local control, taxes, raping the environment. Our officers are jittery. One of them even told me to shove it!"

"How'd he pronounce it?" asked Bentley.

"TUGWOS!"

"Oh my God!"

Bentley bolted out of the room, raced up the three flights to the Oval Office, and barged in. Haig was doing push-ups. "This better be important," he said icily.

"It's happened again, sir. It's Montana this time. Another TUGWOS! They seem to be declaring themselves independent of the United States. Taking hostages. No casualties yet, as far as we can tell. They seem to have wide support."

Haig's eyes glowed like sapphires as his face reddened. "Who the hell do they think they are? *I'm in charge.*" But then, suddenly, Haig's broad shoulders collapsed. "No," he said, "I'm not. Get me Mares on the phone."

"I can't. He's gone fishing."

"Now I'm in real trouble," muttered the President of the Former United States.

"We'll keep trying to reach him," said Bentley Bentley.

Bryan and Mares left South America Pond at 2:30 P.M. From Brighton to Burlington they had whooped and cheered as news of the rapidly escalating Montana secession movement came to them over the car radio.

"Ride 'em, cowboy!" yelled Bryan out the window, recalling his (very, very brief) stint as a bull rider in Montana. Mares remembered his own roots in "big sky" country. Both loved the state (now nation!). By the time they pulled up to Mares's house in Burlington, they were jubilant.

No sooner had they got out of the car than Chris called from the porch, "Bill, President Haig is on the phone."

"How come Chris gets to be in the book and my wife, Lee, doesn't?" muttered Bryan.

"Because you don't have a phone, dummy," said Mares. "What does he want?" he yelled.

"It's about Montana! Something about you helping him out. He needs experienced advice. He's desperate. Wants to hire you guys on as consultants at ten thousand dollars a day."

Bryan and Mares looked at each other.

"Tell him to TUGWOS!"